Treasure of Kalidasa Series 03

# KUMAR SHAMBHAVAM
# OR
# THE BIRTH OF WAR-GOD

Treasure of Kalidasa Series 03

# KUMAR SHAMBHAVAM
# OR
# THE BIRTH OF WAR-GOD

**[TRANSLATED INTO ENGLISH]**

**A POEM BY**

**KALIDASA.**

**PUBLISHED BY**
**THE SOCIETY FOR THE RESUSCITATION OF INDIAN LITERATURE.**

GYAN

*Published by*

Gyan Publishing House
5, Ansari Road
Daryaganj, New Delhi-110002
Phone: 011-47034999, 9811692060
E-mail: books@gyanbooks.com

*Distribution Network*
gyanbooks.com
India, USA, Canada, UK, Australia, France



ISBN : 978-81-212-2464-2 (PB)
First Published, 1901

2nd Impression 2021

*Printed at:* Gyan Press, Delhi.



**Treasure of Kalidasa Series 03**
**Kumar Shambhavam of The Birth of War-God**
Author: Kalidasa

# KUMAR SHAMBHAVAM

OR

# THE BIRTH OF WAR-GOD.

[ *TRANSLATED INTO ENGLISH* ]

A POEM BY

## KALIDASA.

—:O:—

PUBLISHED BY

THE SOCIETY FOR THE RESUSCITATION
OF INDIAN LITERATURE.

CALCUTTA:

PRINTED BY H. C. DASS, ELYSIUM PRESS,
*Kashi Ghose's Lane, Beadon Street.*

1901.

# KUMARA SAMBHAVAM.

## CANTO I.

THERE is in the Northern Quarter, the great king of mountains the Himalnya animated by deity, standing as the measuring rod of the earth and having entered the eastern and western seas.

Having turned him into a calf and the mount Meru standing as the milker competent for milking all the mountains caused the earth to milk out glittering jewels and great herbs instructed by Prithu.

It was the source of endless jewels. The snow did not become the destroyer of its beauty. For one fault becomes lost in a multitude of virtues as the stain on the lunar disc becomes lost in the rays of the moon.

It bears on its peak red mineralledness inducing the coquetry and decorations of Apsaras under a mistaken idea of its being evening and by which divisions of clouds were tinged of a red hue. When troubled by rains the Siddhas, after having previously sought the shade on the lower peaks of clouds moving up to the middle part of the mountain, betake themselves to its sunny summits.

In this mountain the hunters track the way of the maned lions by whom elephants had been killed by means of pearls dropped from the concavity of of their claws even without seeing their foot-steps whose bloody stains had been washed off by the melting down of the snow.

In this mountain the barks of the *Bhurja*-tree with characters written on them with red mineral fluid like the red marks on the elephant's trunk become a useful instrument of Vidyadhara fairies in the way of amatory correspondence.

This mountain, filling the hollow parts of rattling bamboos with the wind rising from the mouths of caves, wishes to obtain as it were the position of the supplier of musical tunes of the Kinnaras about to sing high.

In this mountain the scent, by the issue of milk of Sarala trees rubbed against by elephants for assuaging the itching of their temples, perfumes the peaks.

This mountain protects from the sun the darkness adhering to its caves afraid as it were of the day for great persons consider inferior persons taking refuge as their own proteges.

The chamari deer make significant his tittle "king of mountains" by the fan of their hair and handsome by the waving of their tails fair as moonlight.

The air of this mountain, charged with particles of the water-fall of the Ganges by which Devadaru is shaken and by which the peacock's feathers used by the hunters as girdles are agitated, is enjoyed by hunters by whom the deer are sought.

The sun revolving below causes to open or flourish by rays shooting upward the lotuses growing in the lakes over this mountain the residue of which had been plucked by the hands of the seven Rishis.

Observing the productiveness of sacrificial requisites as also its strength capable of supporting the earth the lord of creation himself conferred on it the kingdom of mountains to which were allotted shares in sacrifices.

Himalaya, the friend of Meru, understanding the limits of authority, married for the perpetuation of his family, by the prescribed ceremonial Mena the mental daughter of the Pitris equal to himself and reverenced even by the Munis.

She gave birth to Mainaka who was to marry (afterwards) a serpent damsel and who had formed a friendly tie with the ocean though Vitra's foe Indra the clipper of wings was angry unconscious of the pain of wounds by the thunder-bolt.

On account of her father Daksha insulting her husband the former wife of Bhava, the chaste Sati, having given up her body by means of Yoga, betook herself to the wife of the mountain for a fresh birth.

That blessed Sati was begotten by the king of mountains on her Menaka intent on holy devotion and undefiled by reason of entire application to sacred observances as success is produced in morals by virtue of enterprise.

Her birth-day, on which all the quarters were clear with the wind clear of dust and a shower of flowers following the blowing of konches, came to pass for the comfort of embodied persons or organic living creatures, moveable or immoveable.

The mother, by means of her daughter resplendent with a halo of light, shone as lands by the side of Mount Vidura shining by means of jewel ribs springing up from the roaring of fresh clouds.

Having received birth she grew up in handsome limbs like the lunar line with other increments of the moon contained in the moon-light itself.

By the patronymic Parvati derived from the mountain, her father, her relations called her who was dear to them. Being forbidden by the mother to practise austerities by means of the words "U má" *oh dont* the hand-some faced girl afterwards got the additional name Umâ.

The eye of the mountain, though having a son in that child, did not get satiety as in mango blossoms of the spring with endless flowers a collection of black bees has great attachment.

As a lamp by a very luminous flame, as the way of heaven by the three-coursed Mandakini, as a scholar by refined or gramatically rectified speech so he was by her, both purified and adored.

With altars of Mandakini's sand, with balls, with artificial pet sons *i.e.* dolls she often played. Being in the midst of her maids a taste for sports grew up as it were in childhood.

As rows of swans come to the Ganges in the autumn, as its own light comes at night to the great orb, so on her, of stable education at the time of education all the intellectual acquisitions of a former existence came.

She adorned with unartificial ornament got into the age following infancy *i.e.* youth, the instrument of hilarity without what is called intoxicating liquor and the weapon of Kama without flowers.

Her body, symmetrically developed by fresh youth, became handsome in all parts like a painting touched up by a fresh brush.

By the lustre of the raised toe and nail and from setting the feet her two feet, emitting as it were redness, assumed the splendour of the land lotus moving about.

With the body somewhat stooping in gait affected by sportive gestures she was instructed by swans coveting instruction in turn and desirous of receiving the beautiful sound of anklets.

Having a waist like the middle of an altar the

young lady held three beautiful streaks placed in a ladder.

This is my inference that her two arms, more tender than the *Sirisha* flower, though worsted by Kamadeva whose symbal was a fish, were like cords for encircling the neck of Hara.

The unstable goddess of Fortune and beauty when got to the moon does not enjoy the excellences of the lotus [which is supposed to close at night] and again when she gets to the lotus she does not obtain lunar splendour. But getting to Uma's face she received the two fold delight both of the moon and the lotus. If a flower could have been contained in a fresh leaf, if a pearl could have been in a transparent coral then it might have imitated her fair smile beautified with red lips.

To her speaking with a voice distilling nectar even a *kokila*, nurtured by strange birds, appears hoarse-sounding to the hearer like a discordant instrument being struck.

The unstable look, not different from a blue lotus affected by a strong breeze, was received by her, the large-eyed, from female deer or was it received from her by the female deer.

Seeing the beauty of her two long-curved eye-brows as if produced by a pencil with black paint and expert in action Kamadeva gave up pride of beauty for his own bow.

If in the mind of the irrational animals there were or could be a feeling of shame then doubtless the Chamari deer, seeing the collection of hair of the daughter of the mountain king, would make slack their fondness for hair.

By the whole collection of examplar substances, each in its own respective place, having been placed assiduously by the creator of the universe she was made as if from a desire on the part of the creator of seeing beauty concentrated in one place.

Narada, rambling at pleasure, having seen that damsel near her father, declared that she would be the one wife, possessing half the body, by love, of Siva.

Though her age was mature yet the father remained averse from the desire of having any other bride-groom than Siva for his daughter, for excepting fire other heats do not deserve the ghee consecrated by Mantras.

The mountain was not able to make or ask the God Siva himself not suing, to receive his daughter for fear of the request failing. A noble person takes to indifference even in a wished-for object.

From the very time when in her former birth the fine-teethed damsel gave up her body because of Daksha's anger, the lord of brutes Siva, forsaking all attachments, remained unmarried.

The skin-clothed Siva, of a restrained spirit, dwelt for ascetic meditation, on a certain peak of the Himalaya mountain wherein the Devadaru trees were washed by the streams of the Ganga and where the musk-scented Kinnaras sang.

Siva's followers, having Nameru flowers in their vests, clothed in the bark of the Bhurja, tender to the feet, ornamented with red arsenic, sat on the surface of rocks abounding in fragrant resin.

The humped bull, proudly bellowing but with an agreeable voice and bruising by the points of his hoofs solid rocks of snow seen with difficulty by the terrified Gavaya deer and unable to endure the lion's roar, bellowed.

The eight-formed Siva, having there set up a fire lighted by sacrificial wood, another of his own forms, himself the dispenser of the fruits of asceticism, practised asceticism actuated by some desire which none could guess.

Having worshipped the price-less who was worshipped of the dwellers of heaven with offerings the lord of mountains directed his devoted daughter accompanied by her maids to serve him.

Siva permitted her to serve him though her attractions were calculated to be an impediment to mental abstraction. They alone are firm whose minds are not perturbed on there being a cause of perturbation.

The fine-haired damsel Parvati, plucking flowers for offering, expert in cleaning the altar, and bringing waters for the daily rites and kusa grass, worshipped him, her labor alleviated by the rays of the moon on Siva's head.

---

## CANTO II.

Oppressed by the Asura Tara, the dwellers of heaven, with Indra at their head, went to the residence of Brahma.

Brahma manifested himself to them the beauty of whose faces had faded like the sun appearing in the morning over lakes whose lotuses were closed.

They all, having bowed, addressed the creator of all who had heads on four sides, the lord of speech, with significant words.

"Salutation to thee, three-formed, existing as one spirit before creation but afterwards betaking to distinctive forms for the separation of three qualities Sattwa, Rajas and Tamas.

O thou uncreate, the seed sown by thee in the midst of waters is not fruitless for therein is produced the universe, moveable and immoveable. Thou, its cause, art sung.

Manifesting thy glory by three forms thou alone holdest the causeship of destruction, conservation and creation. Male and female are but parts of thy body who wert divided in two forms by desire of creation. They themselves are held as parents of the creation.

Of thee whose night and day are divided by the

measure of thy own time, sleeping and walking are but the destruction and creation of all creatures.

Thou art the cause of the universe, thyself causeless——thou the end of the universe theyself endless——thou the beginning of the universe, thyself without beginning——thou the lord of the universe, thyself lordless.

Thou knowest thyself by thy own act, thou createst thy form in thyself by thy own act, dost thou absorb thyself in thyself.

Thou art liquid, thou also solid hard, thou art gross, thou also subtle, thou art light and thou art heavy; thou art also perfectly developed and thou undeveloped, according to thy own desire in the atomic and other forms at thy command.

Of those sentences whose first syllable is *Om*, whose pronounciation is by the three accents, whose ordinance is sacrifice and whose ritualistic fruit is heaven thou art the cause.

They call thee Prakriti or nature engaging in the act of creation for the purposes of *Purusha* or soul. They know theyself also to be the *Purusha* or soul, sitting apart and looking on Prakriti.

Thou art father even of the fathers, God even of Gods. Thou art superior even of superiors, creator even of Prajapatis.

Thyself art even the sacrificial offering ghee, also the sacrifice, the object enjoyed and the enjoyer—the everlasting. Thou art the object of knowledge and also the knower, the meditator and the supreme object of meditation"

Having heard these laudatory expressions from them, true and agreeable the creator, being inclined to grace the Gods, replied

Uttered by the four mouths of that primeval poet the four fold utterance of sounds was successful

" O ye great powers, welcome to you who having by your authority held your own rights have at once taken possession by your long arms

What is this? Why your faces do not possess as before your own light like stars whose light has been enfeebled by frost

By the extinction of the flame the thunderbolt of the destrover of Vitra, not emitting the divine weapon, appears contracted in the corners

Irresistable by the enemy the noose in the hand of Varuna has betaken to the miserable plight of a serpent bereft of its energy by incantations

Kuvera's arm, destitute of its club, like a tree whose branches have broken down, declares as it were his defeat like a javelin sticking in his heart Yama also marking the ground by his staff, its spendour gone to ruin, imparts the smallness of an exinguished fire brand to this his staff though at one time never failing

Why these Adityas, cold by the destruction of their fiery energy like paintings, have got to the condition of being gazed upon at pleasure,

From the revolving instability of the winds their stoppage of onward velocity is inferred like the stoppage of a stream of water from the incursión of an ópposite stream.

The heads of the Rudras too having the Innar curves pendent on the downcast crests of clotted hair are declaring the loss of hunkara.

Having once gained place, have you been made to turn back by stronger enemies as in jurisprudence, eithics, grammar &c a general rule or law is made to submit to special legislation or exception.

Ȯ my sons, what do you all so earnestly ask for from myself having come in a body? In me is the office-of the creation of the worlds and in you is placed the office of their preservation.

Indra, with his thousand eyes beautiful like the lotus shaken by the gentle breeze, moved Vrihaspati, the preceptor of Gods.

Vrihaspati, the lord of speech, who though only two-eyed was wiser than the thousand and two-eyed Indra, with palms joined said this to the lotus-seated Brahma.

"True what you say, our rights have been overturned by enemies. Yourself inhering in every person how O Lord, thou knowest it not.

Elated with the boon obtained from you the great Asura, by name Taraka, has got up like a comet for the oppression of the worlds.

The sun spreads only so much heat in his town

by which alone the opening of the lotus in his tank is accomplished.

The moon serves him always with all his digits. He does not take only that line which has become the crest jem of Hara or Siva.

The wind, desisting from its course in his garden from fear of the consequences of theft or blowing off of any flowers, does not blow more than the air excited by the fan by his side.

The six seasons having given up attendance in gradation serve him each in its turn like gardeners bent on collecting flowers.

The lord of rivers with great labour watches jewels fit for presents within the waters until maturity.

The serpents with Vasuki as their leader, with crest jems glittering on their hoods, having got at night the state of fixed lamps serve him around.

Indra also, looking for acts of grace from him, propitiates him with the ornaments of the desire-fulfilling tree presented by means of ambassadors.

Though he is thus served yet he opposes the three worlds for the wicked can only be moderated by injuries in return not by benefits.

The trees of Indra's Nandana gardens whose leaves were gently plucked by the hands of the celestial women are being felled by him.

He is fanned when asleep by chouries exciting wind only like breaths, showering drops of tears of captive goddesses.

Having plucked off peaks of Meru beaten by the troops of the sun's horses hills for amusement have been formed by him in his own mansions.

Of Mandakini the waters soiled by the temporal juice of the quarters are the only residuum ; of the golden lotuses their produce his tanks are now the only repository.

Pleasure on surveying the worlds is not felt by the gods, the way of their chariots having become waste from fear of his incursion.

The enchanter snatches away the ghee afforded by priests in sacrifices that are held. We see it in our very sight from fire's mouth.

The great Uchchaisrava of Indra, that jewel of a horse, has been siezed by him like the glory acquired from a long time set in Indra's person.

All our measures against the murderous Asura have been baffled in their effects like powerful medicines in a malignant congestive fever.

Our hope of victory by Hari's quoit, its lustre rising by the re-action of the stroke, lies as a breast plate fixed to his neck.

His elephants by which the Airavata (cloud-elephant) was defeated now lie in clouds swollen with abundant water and repeat strokes on the surface.

O Lord, we desire to create a General for his destruction as persons desirous of emancipation seek, for the cessation of the world, the righteousness which cuts assunder the bondage of works, having placed in front which defender of the divine troops the cutter of mountains, Indra, shall bring back from the enemy the Fortune of victory like a captive."

On the termination of that speech the self-existent Brahma made a speech which excelled by its felicitousness the rain which succeeds thunder.

"This your desire shall be accomplished. Have a little patience. But in the matter of this General I shall not engage personally in the business of his creation.

From myself that demon has become possessed of Fortune and therefore from myself he ought not to have destruction again. Even one should not cut off himself a poisonous tree after having reared it.

This itself was asked by him of yore and it was promised by me. For by means of a boon his ascetic meditation which was able to consume the world was destroyed by me.

Who can withstand him engaged in war himself a war-like person except a portion of Siva's substance?

That god is the supreme luminary, beyond the quality of Tamas. He is not comprehensible in his dignity and greatness by me or by Vishnu.

Do you, that seek a remedy, labour to attract the mind of Sambhu absorbed in ascetic contemplation by the beauty of Uma like iron by a magnet.

The two alone are able to bear the energy of us

two, Sambhu's and mine. Either she, Uma to bear Sambhu's or his watery form to bear mine.

Having obtained your General from black-necked Siva he shall liberate the branded locks of the captive Goddesses by the amplitude of his energy or power."

Having thus addressed the gods the cause of the universe Brahma vanished. The gods too, fixed in mind about what they should do, went to heaven.

Having fixed on Kamdeva as the proper agent the chastiser of the demon Paka Indra remembered him with a mind doubly swift from his haste in the accomplishment of the object.

The flower-bowed Kamdeva, whose weapon the mango-blossom was deposited in the hands of his companion the spring, having attached his bow the beautiful extremeties of which were set with eye-brow creepers of handsome female,to his neck marked by the bracelet of his wife Rati, attended on him.

——:o:——

## CANTO III.

HAVING left the gods thousand eyes of Indra fell simultaneously on Kamadeva because of its depenance on an object; the regard of masters is generally unstable in their dependants.

Being allowed room near the throne by Vasava and having acknowledged his master's grace by bowing his head he began to speak thus secretly to him.

"O thou that knowest the excellences of all men, command us what thou wouldst to be done in these worlds. I wish thy favour excited by thy remembrance of me be extended into a command.

By what person ambitious of dignity by means of excessively long asceticisms thy jealousy has been begotten? For he shall soon become subject to the influence of this my bow to which the arrow is set.

Let him, who from fear of repeated existence but against thy will has betaken to the way of emancipation, remain long bound by glances of women with amorous movements of the eye-brows.

Say, the wealth and virtue of which thy foe though taught morals by Sukra himself shall the agent of infused morality injure like rapid currents the two shores of a river.

Say what female austerely following out her bow of having one husband only but because of her beauty entered into thy unstable mind thou desirest to have released from modesty and of her own accord taking hold of thee with her arm around thy neck?

Be propitous O hero, let thy thunder-bolt rest. By means of my arrows any foe of the gods whoever he be, the p wer of his arm being rendered futile, shall fear even women with their under lips swelling with rage.

By thy grace though I am armed only with

flowers, having got only one helper in the spring I shall make a failure of patience even of Hara who has the pinaka bow in hand; what are other bowmen in comparison."

Having taken down his foot from his thigh and honouring the footstool by resting on it Indra thus spoke to Kama who had asserted his power in the designed object that is of attracting the heart of Siva.

"Oh friend, all this is accomplished in thee; both are my weapons the thunder-bolt and yourself. The thunder-bolt is ineffectual in those who are powerful by force of asceticism, but you as a weapon can both go on all sides and are also affective.

I know thy strength. I shall employ thee equal to myself in a heavy work. Having observed his habit of sustaining the earth the chief of serpents is appointed by Krishna for holding his body.

By thee declaring the course of arrow to reach Siva whose mark is a bull our work is almost accomplished already. Understand this itself is the desired object of Gods enjoying shares in sacrifices but now having enemies.

These gods wish for a General begotten of Siva's energy for their victory. Siva too can be managed only by the cast of thy one arrow for he, the repositary of the members of mantras, being now fixed in spirit in his own essence.

By the direction of her father the daughter of the

king of mountains is serving Siva practicing ascecticism on a high land. This has been heard by me from the mouth of Apsaras for that class are my emissaries. Therefore go for the accomplishment of this business of the gods. This object to be encompassed by another cause that is the presence of Parvati, requires thee as its ultimate cause as the seed and the sprout requires water before production.

Thine is the use of the weapons in that means for the victory of the gods for thou art the successful agent. Even a work of no note which requires one peculiar talent is for the glory of men.

These gods are the petitioners, the business is of the three worlds, and the work to be done by thy bow is not very hurtful. Oh thou art of a wonderful and enviable power.

The spring too, Oh destroyer of the spirit, from his companionship with you though not spoken to is thy helper. Charge the wind saying become the exciter of fire.

Saying "so be it" Kama having received his master's command as a holy residuum went away. Indra touched his body by his hand rendered rough by driving the Airavat.

Followed by the spring his dear friend and by his wife Rati and determined to accomplish the requested business even at the loss of his body Kama went with fear to the hermitage of Siva in the Himalaya.

Having assumed his own form the source of pride unto Kama, the spring, hostile to fixed austere contem-templation of the ascetic Munis, appeared in that forest.

The sun being bent on going unseasonably to the quarter in the keeping of Kuvera, the North the Southern quarter, by its face, discharged air like a sigh of sorrow.

The Asoka tree produced at once flowers with leaves commencing from the trunk itself and did not wait for a stroke of the feet of females sounding with anklets.

The spring set black bees, the characters as it were of Kama's name, on arrow-like fresh mango blossoms with young leaves produced at once as feathers getting completion.

Notwithstanding the excellence of colour the Kar-nikara flower, distresed, offended the mind by its un-scentedness. The inclination of the Creator of the universe becomes generally averse to the collection of all virtues in one subject.

The excessively red Palasa flowers, curved like a young moon because of being unblown, appeared like wounds from nails just inflicted on the forest sites coming together with the spring.

The beauty of the spring having put forth at the outset the Tilaka flower as a mark of beauty varie-gated by adhering black bees as a black paint, adorned by the orient sun as a red tincture and with young mango blossoms for her lips.

Being obstructed in their view by particles of dust of the flower stalk of Piyala trees the deer, buoyant with hilarity, ranged about against the winds over the forest plains resounding with the fall of old leaves.

The sounds which the male Kokila, with the neck red from the taste of the mango sprouts, gave out sweetly became the speech of Kama able to counteract the sensitiveness of virtuous women.

The rise of perspiration of Kinnara women, with clear nether lips and the color of the face slightly yellowish because of the decline of cold, made a footing on the painted writings of the body.

On seeing the untimely rise of spring the ascetics dwelling in Siva's forest became with difficulty controllers of their minds and prevented with labor their perterbation.

Madana, with his flower-bow stringed and Rati for his companion, having reached that region, both orders of creatures indicated by their acts a state pervaded by the sentiment of attachment having reached its maximum. In one flower vessel the black-bee drank honey following his own beloved mate. The black deer stratched by his born the female deer, her eyse closed by his touch.

The female elephant gave out of love to the male elephant a mouthful of warte scented with the lotus dust. The Chakrabaka, named after the part of a carriage *viz.*, wheel, treated his wife with a lotus stalk half-devoured.

In the intervals of singing the Kinnara kissed his wife's face the painting on 'which was a little washed off by drops of perspiration and bedecked by eyes rolling a little by the effect of liquors.

Even the trees received, from their wives the creepers, having large clusters of flowers and beautified with resplendant young red leaves as their lips, the entwining embrace of their bending branch-arms.

Though hearing the songs of Apsaras at that time Siva became bent on spiritual contemplation for obstructions can never interrupt the fixed devotion of those who can keep under control their minds.

Going to the door of the creeper-house Nandi, with a golden rod placed in his left hand, directed by the sign of the fore-finger placed on the mouth, Siva's troops not to disturb.

By Nandi's command the whole forest, with trees unshaken, black bees still, 'the birds silent and the deer stopped ranging, remained like an effort transferred to painting *i.e.* like a landscape.

Avoiding the range of his sight like a place with Venus in front on setting out on a journey Kama entered by sides the place of meditation of Siva covered by the branches of Nameru trees.

He, whose body was on the verge of destruction, saw the self-controlled three-eyed Siva sitting on an altar of Devadaru tree with a tiger-skin laid over it.

He was sitting in the *Virasana* posture with the fore half of his body still, perpendicular and large, with both shoulders bent and because of the two hands being placed with the concave of the palms upward like a full blown lotus in the bosom.

His clotted hair was tied up with snakes; double strings of rosaries were fixed to his ears and he wore a hide of black deer darkened still more by the reflection of his black throat.

He had three eyes almost closed in meditation, not frowning, untwinkling, looking downward and observing the nose.

He was sitting like a cloud without an effort of rain, like a reservoir of waters in which there was no wave upheaving from the stoppage of inward vital airs, like an unshaken flame in a place where there is no wind.

By means of the rays of light getting a way through the third eye in the cranium and issuing from the crown of the head was obscured the beauty, more tender than the fibres of the lotus stalk, of the crescent on Siva's head.

Having fixed in the heart the mind controlled by meditation restricted from action through nine doors *i.e.* having no communication with external world he was beholding the spirit in himself whom persons conversant with knowledge subjective know.

Seeing from a short distance the three eyed Siva in that state beyond the ken of thought Kama, his head trembling through fear, did not perceive that the bow and arrow dropped from his own hand.

As if restoring his power which was on the verge of destruction by the beauty of her body there appeared the daughter the king of mountains followed by two forest-goddesses.

She was carrying ornaments of spring flowers which by means of Asoka flower left in the shade the ruby, wherein the Karnikar flowers had appropriated the splendour of gold and in which the Sindhuvara had become like a collection of pearls.

Wearing an orient-red garment she was stooping a little by the weight of her rising breast like a walking creeper with leaves bent down by clusters of flowers.

With eyes unstable from fear she was warding off every moment by a toy lotus a black bee, whose thirst was excited by her perfumed sweet breath, flying near her nether lip red as *Vimb*.

Seeing her unblemished in all her limbs and more handsome than Rati the flower-bannered Kama again expected the success of his undertaking in the self-restrained spear-holder Siva.

Uma too approached the site of the door of her future husband Sambhu. He was absorbed in delight by seeing within by meditation the chief light styled supreme spirit.

The lord, whose site was with difficulty held below by the extremeties of the hood of the king of serpents, having gradually set the vital airs at liberty, slackened the hard meditative posture in which he had sat.

Having bowed down Nandi announced to him that the daughter of the mountain had come for doing service and admitted her whose admission was allowed by a mere sign of the eye-brow.

The collection of spring flowers plucked by her own hands mixed with parts of stalks were scattered by her two companions over the feet of Siva.

Uma too, dropping the fresh Karnikara flower which was resplendent amid her dark locks, made a bow with her head whereof leaves dropped from the ear by the very act of bowing to Siva whose emblem was a bull.

Siva's benediction on Uma's bowing down before him was "obtain a husband not having another wife." She was indeed told a truth by Siva. The sayings of great personages never cherish an unreal signification.

Kama, watching the fit time for his arrow, desirous of entering like a grasshopper the mouth of the fire, fixing his aim at Hara in the presence of Uma, touched the bow string.

Gouri then offered to the mountain dweller Sīva, by a hand red as copper, a wreath of the seeds of the lotus of the river Mandakini dried by the rays of the sun.

As soon as out of the respect to the offerer the three-eyed Siva was about to accept the wreath the flower-bannered applied a never-failing arrow by name Fascination to his bow.

His firmness a little lost like the ocean at the commencement of the moon's rise fixed his three eyes on the face of Uma with lips like the fruit vimb.

Betraying sentiment by her limbs resplendent like a young Kadamva the daughter of the mountain stood bending and flushing with a very handsome face, the eyes cast down through bashfulness.

Having again strongly restrained the distraction of his senses by virtue of his self-control and desiring to discover the cause of the perturbation of his mind he cast his sight at the corners of the four quarters.

Siva saw Kama with his fist clenched at the corner of the right eye, his shoulder bent, his left leg contracted and his handsome bow stretched circularly attempting to strike.

From the third eye of him increased in rage at the attack against his devotion and having a face difficult to look at owing to the contraction of his brows a flaming fire suddenly issued out.

"O lord, refrain, refrain thy anger." While these words of the gods were passing in the sky that ire, produced from Siva's eyes, turned Kama into a residuum of ashes.

The operation of the senses being stopped by a delusion produced by a sharp discomfiture and gnorant of her husband's destruction Rati was benefitted as it were, by being for a moment stunned.

Having quickly destroyed him, the obstruction of asceticism as the thunder-bolt breaks a tree, the ascetic Siva, desiring to avoid the vicinity of women, vanished with his troops.

Considering that the desire of her father that she should be Siva's wife had become futile and with her handsome body becoming more bashful in the presence of two companions she went on with dejected face homeward.

Immediately having received by his two arms his pitiable daughter her eyes closed by fear of Rudra's rage like the celestial elephant, supporting the lotus adhering to his tusk the mountain became one that follows way wherever it might lead having his form enlarged by his haste.

———:o:———

## CANTO IV.

The wife of Kama, being in a fainting feet and motionless, was restored to sense by Providence willing to make her feel her new state of widow-hood which was intolerable to the feeling.

She made her two eyes which had opened at the end of her fit intent on observing things around her. She did not know that the darling object of those two never satiated eyes had become utterly lost to sight.

Saying "O thou lord of my life, art thou living?" and getting up she saw before her on the ground a human figure turned into ashes by the fire of Siva's rage. Again distracted, her bosom becoming of a brown hue by rolling on the ground and her hairs scattered she bewailed making the forest site as it were equally distressed with herself.

"This that thy body which was the sampler by its beautifulness of gay persons has fallen into such a state yet I am not not lacireted. Oh women are hard.

Having cast aside me whose life is dependent on thee, having in a moment broken through thy friendship where art thou fled like a collection of water with embankments broken down rushing out leaving behind the lotus whose life is dependent on itself.

Thou hast not ever done anything displeasing to me nor has anything adverse to thee been done by me. Why then is not thy sight granted without any cause to Rati who is bewailing thee.

Is it, oh Smara, that thou rememberest my binding thee with the waist band on names of some rival dropping from thy lips in unconscious moments or my beating thee with the ornament lotus by which thine eyes would be injured from the dropping pollen of the flower.

To please me thou wouldst say "thou dwellest in my heart." I perceive it now to be a pretext. If this were not a mere complementary saying how is it that thou art destitute of body and Rati is uninjured.

I shall on my part take to thy way who art a new sojourner in the other world. But this world is defrauded by fate for happinees of embodied beings is indeed dependent on thee.

The roads of the city being veiled by the darkness of the night who, oh dear, except thee is able to make the females distracted by the roar of clouds to reach the residence of their friends.

Thou being non-existent the intoxication of wine turning the eyes red and causing words to slip at every step is now but a mere farce on the part of jolly women.

Oh thou bodyless, having learnt that his dear friend's body is turned into a mere word the moon whose rise will now be fruitless on the dark fortnight passing away will give up his waning with regret.

Say whose arrow shall the fresh mango blossoms with beautiful yellow and red petiole brought to notice by the melodious voice of the male Kokila become.

This row of black bees employed many times by thee to do duty as a bow string now condoles with me heavily afflicted by means of humming in piteous tones.

O thou versed in love, this ornament of the flowers of season set by thee on my limbs is still held but that handsome body of thine is not seen.

Before the decoration (dying) of my left foot was finished thou wert called away by the cruel God. Do thou make my left foot now red.

By voluntarily burning myself as a Sati I will again become a refugee in your bosom while, O dear, you are not coveted in heaven by the artful females of the Gods.

Even though I may follow thee my lasting shame will be that I have lived one moment after thee.

Thyself being separated from me in the other world how could I finish the last decoration ? Thou hast incurred an unexpected condition at once with thy body and thy life.

I remember thy smiling discourse with the spring and the glance in the corner of thy eye whilst thou wert making thy arrow straight and the bow was being attached to thy arrow.

Where is thy bosom friend the spring who had prepared thy bow with flowers ; he has not been made to incur by the fierce holder of pinaka the condition."

Having been wounded in his heart by those bewailing expressions of Rati as it were by arrows besmeared with poison the spring appeared before her to condole with her in her affliction.

Seeing him she cried exceedingly and pressing her breasts struck her chest for sorrow increases before an intimate friend or relative.

Afflicted she addressed him thus " See, O Spring, what is the state of your friend. This heap of ashes variegated like a pigeon in small particles is scattered by the winds.

O Kama, grant now a sight of yourself. This spring wishes to see you. The love of men is indeed unstable in their wives but it is not certainly in their friend.

Was not the universe including gods and demons made by this thy friend to do the command of thy bow whose string was lotus stalk fibres and whose arrows were delicate flowers.

Thy friend is gone. He will not return like a amp struck out by the wind. I am like his wick. See me smoking by intolerable distress.

In the murder of Kama by fate leaving me is not a half-murder done? On the secure refuge-tree being broken down by an elephant the creeper must drop down.

Therefore do this service immediately to a friend. By applying fire make me reach the vicinity of my husband.

The moon-light goes with the moon, the lightning is dissolved with the cloud. That women go the way of their husbands is understood even by those of little sense.

Having painted my breasts by this auspicious heaps of ashes of my beloved husband's body as in bed of new leaves I shall place my body in the fire.

O excellent friend, in the flower-bed you have often been a companion to us both. Make now soon likewise my funeral pile being petitioned by my bowing with palms joined,

After that question set the fire to me by blowing the south wind. It is certainly known to thee how my husband Kama is not for one moment cheered without me.

Having done this, offer, to us two, one doubled palmful of water. Without dividing it in the other world thy friend will drink it with me.

O spring, in ceremonies for the other world, offer clusters of mango blossoms with tender leaves for thy friend for he is fond of them."

A voice from the sky tenderly addressed Rati thus determined in giving up her body as a first shower shows pity on the fish Saphari distressed by the drying up of the pond.

"O thou wife of the flower-armed, thy husband will not long remain unattainable to thee. Hear by what work he got into the condition of a moth in the flame of Siva's eye.

Prompted by his senses, the lord of creation Brahma felt a desire for her own daughter. Then having suppressed his mental perversion he cursed

Kama who in consequence thereof has experienced this.

When Siva shall marry Parvati being inclined to her by virtue of her asceticism then obtaining happiness he shall join Kama to his body.

Asked by Dharma Brahma spoke thus the word setting limit to the malediction against Kama. For the self restrained and clouds are productive causes both of lightning and of nectar.

O thou of beautiful face, preserve this body in which there will be a reunion with thy husband for the river whose waters have been drunk off by the sun at the close of summer is again joined by streams.

In this manner some creature of an invisible form prevented Rati's thought of bringing on death. And by faith in that voice the friend of the flower bannered the Spring comforted her by words well-composed.

Then thinned by sorrow the wife of Kama remained expecting the termination of her misfortune as the curve of the diurnal moon obscured by the fading of its rays expects the evening.

---

## CANTO V.

Kama being burnt in her presence by Siva, Parvati, being baffled in her wishes, reproached her beauty in her mind for hadsomeness is only a desirable accomplishment as productive of graciousness in husbands.

She wished to render beauty fruitful by practising fixed devotion by means of asceticisms. How else can these two be obtained *viz.*, such love as she subsequently found in Siva and such a husband too?

Having heard of her daughter prepared for asceticism, whose mind was set on Siva, the lord of mountains, Mena, embracing her by the chest and dissuading her from the great vow fit only for a Muni, spoke to her.

Worship at home the deities desired by the mind. Where O child is asceticism and where is thy body? The tender Sirisha flower may endure the footsteps of the black bee but not of a bird.

Thus exhorting her daughter of firm purpose Mena was not able to restrain her from her undertaking. Who can oppose the mind resolutely set on its desired object or water inclining downwards?

At a certain time, she, fixed as she was by the mouth of a competent intimate maid, asked of her father permission to retire from home into the forests for ascetic devotion to last until the issue of its object.

Permitted by her revered father who was pleased with her suitable determination Gauri went to a peak full of peacocks, which was among the people afterwards called after her Gauri-peak.

Having cast aside her wreath of pearls by the waiving of whose string the sandal-paste had been wiped off she, fixed in her resolve, wore a waist coat of barks of trees twany like a young sun.

As her face had been lovely by her decorated hair so it became by her clotted hair, as a lotus becomes resplendent not only by rows of black bees, but also by contact with moss or weeds.

The votaress was tied with zone of grass which reddened the fair form it girdled round. Never before the Lady's waist had felt the ceaseless pain of such a rough belt.

Her hand, not employed in the decoration of her lower lip now giving up its red hue and not requiring hand to apply ornamenting lip salve and from the ball reddened by the painting of the bosom of which the fingers were bruised by contact with Kusa grass, was made by her a companion of the rosary.

She, who was troubled even by the flowers in her tresses dropped by her turning on a costly bed, now slept making an arm her pillow and sitting down on the bare ground.

Two things were deposited by her engaged in ascetic exercises with two parties with a view to take them back; one was lovely motion in tender creepers, the other was rolling look in the female deer.

Herself unsleeping she nourished the small trees with the liquid issue of her jar-breasts her first-born maternal affection for whom even Kartikeya would not be able to counteract.

Even the deer, nourished by grants of handfuls

of wild grain, had such confidence in her as that by their eyes she measured the eyes of her maids in front of herself.

Even the Munis went to see her, having gone through ablutions, made the fire offering and put on the garment of barks. In those who have grown up in religion age is not taken into account.

And that hermitage became sanctifying in which the injurious animals had given up their former noxiousness, in which guests were served by trees with their desired fruits and in which the sacred fire was collected in the new leaf huts.

When by the exercise of asceticism at first undertaken she considered the desired fruit unattainable then not reckoning the tenderness of her body she commenced to practise severe asceticism.

She, who got fatigued even by playing with dolls, entered into severe asceticism. Surely her body was made of golden lotus by nature both tender as lotus and strong as gold.

Having got into the midst of four blazing fires and having overcome the solar light dazzling to the eyes the fine-waisted damsel, smiling delightedly, used to gaze at the sun in summer looking at nothing else.

Her face, thus heated by the rays of the Sun, got the splendour of the lotus which opens when the sun shines. Only at the large eye corners a site was gradually obtained by blackness.

Rain and nectareous moon was her ordained sustenance, a livelihood not otherwise than that of a tree which lives on light, air and rain.

Excessively heated by a five-fold fire, one from the sky *i.e.* the sun and four others on her four sides from the burning fuel and having been washed with fresh waters *i.e.* the rain at the close of the summer she let off heat together with the heated earth.

The first drops of water, standing for a moment on the eye-lashes, striking the lower lip, then dashing on the swollen bosom and then dropping by sides, got after a long time to the navel.

The nights, with lightning looks, saw her sleeping on a rock, unhoused and in the midst of uninterrupted rain and storm, remaining as it were the witness of her great asceticism.

Remaining in the water and taking pity on the couple of Chakravakas seperated before her and crying to one another she passed the nights of Pous in which the winds were producing excessive frosts.

By a mouth lotus-scented at night and the lower lips quaking from cold and exhibiting the beauty of lotus leaf she made as it were a furnishing of lotus for the waters deprived of their supply of lotuses by showers of frost.

Living on leaves of trees dropped off themselves is of itself the highest degree of asceticism. But by her even that nourishment was refused.

Afflicting day and night by such vows her own

body tender as lotus fibres she greatly excelled the asceticism of ascetics acquired by bodies capable of enduring trouble.

Then a certain person, with clotted hair, clad in deer skin, holding a staff, bold in speech and shining as it were with Vedic light, entered the hermitage, the first stage of Brahmanical life endued as it were with a body.

With very respectful adoration the hospitable Parvati advanced to receive him. Even where there is equality the great persons become excessively attentive in acts of homage and civility.

Having accepted the adoration offered according to rule and rested a while he, looking at Uma with upright eyes, began to speak incoherently.

Are wood and Kusa grass for sacrificial acts easily obtainable and waters fit for thy ablution? Dost thou engage in asceticism in adaptation to thy own strength? Forsooth the body is the first requisite for religious works.

Are the clusters of creepers grown by waters supplied by thee thriving? They rise to equality with thy lower lip, which though long bereft of red-dying is still red.

Is thy mind at ease with the deer which seize from attachment the sacrificial grass in thy hands and which, O lotus-eyed, by their rolling eyes claim equality with thy eyes.

Men say, O Parvati, that a handsome appearance

does not tend to sin. That saying is true for thy virtue, O thou with large eyes, has got to the position of instructing regular Munis.

This mountain with his race was not so sanctified by the waters of the Ganges fallen from the sky smiling with the showered offering of the seven Rishis as by thine unstained acts.

Hereby virtue appears, more especially now to me, the most excellent of the three objects *viz.*, virtue, wealth and desire, since it is, O thou of excellent thoughts, served by thee of whose mind wealth and desire are no objects.

You ought not to consider me a stranger thus highly honoured by yourself since O thou that stoopest with thy body, the meeting of good persons is itself described by the wise as friendship contracted by the utterance of seven words.

From the very nature of a Brahmin being disposed to loquacity this person is desirous of asking something of you, so forbearing. O thou lady ascetic, if it be not a secret thou oughtest to answer me.

Your birth is in the race of the Primival Brahma. Your body is the concentration of the beauty of the three worlds. You have every enjoyment already and are youthful. Then what better fruit of asceticism can there be?

From some intolerable grievance there may possibly be such an ascetic disposition in high-minded ladies. But on reflection I see that such a case does not appear in you, O thou of a slender frame.

This thy frame is incapable of incurring grief or disregard. How, O thou with beautiful eye-brows, could there be any disrespect in thy father's house? There can be no stranger's attack on you. Who could extend his hand for taking the jem on a serpent's hood?

Why it is that in youth having cast away ornaments, barks of trees suitable for old age are worn by thee? Say, if the night, with the moon and stars shining, is intended for Aruna, the sun's charioteer.

If thou desirest heaven thy labor is uselesss for thy father's territories are divine sites. And if thou desire a bride-groom away with ascetic devotion for a jewel does not seek an acceptor. It is sought by the would-be recipient.

Your desire for a bridegroom is made known by a warm breath or sigh. But still my mind falls into doubt for no one appears worthy of your desire. How can there be a desired person who is unattainable?

Oh there is some stern youth desired by thee who disregards thy clotted hair hanging loosely on thy cheeks, long destitute of ear lotuses and twany like the extremeties of paddy.

What sentient man's mind is not afflicted who sees thee exceedingly emaciated by ascetic vows fit only for Munis with thy limbs sun-burnt like the unar carve by day ?

Thy beloved one is self-defrauded by his pride of beauty since he does not come within the sight of thy eye which has an agreeable glance with curved eye-lashes. O Gouri, thou hast been toiling for some time and there is the merit of my asceticism too collected during my primary stage. Therefore by the half of that merit recieve your desired boon of a bride-groom and I wish to know him well.

Thus addressed by the Brahmin penetrating into her inmost thought she was not able to declare her bridegroom's name. She looked, with averted eyes having the black paint defaced, upon her companion remaining at her side.

Her companion said to him :—" Hear, O Brahmacharin, for whom Uma has made her body a means of ascetic practice turning as it were a lotus leaf into a parasol.

Disregarding the highly rich Indra and others, the lords of the four quarters, this lady wishes, with high aspirations, to obtain for her husband the Pinaka-handed Siva who is not subject to personal attractions from the overthrow of Kama.

Turned back by his intolerable fury, the arrow of the flower-bowed Kama, whose body was destroyed, its points not reaching the enemy of the three cities, afflicted this lady with a deep stroke.

Thenceforward remaining love-stricken in her

father's house her curls have become grey by the sandal mark on the forehead; the young lady never obtained any rest not even on the surface of rocks of solid snow.

On the acts of Siva commencing to be sung by means of words dropped from a sobbing throat this lady repeatedly caused the daughters of the king of Kinnaras, her companions in singing, to weep at the extremity of the forest.

Having for a moment closed her two eyes at night of which a third part was yet remaining she would suddenly awake speaking incoherently "O Nilkantha, where are you going?" and throwing her clasped arms on an imaginary neck.

Drawing a picture of the moon-crested Siva in her own hand she would in secret reprove him saying " Since you are by the wise called all-pervading how do you not know this person in a state of love to you?"

When after seeking she did not see any other means of getting the lord of universe, she, by the permission of her father, betook herself to the hermitage in our company for asceticism.

Fruits have appeared in these trees which had been grown by her and have witnessed her asceticism but her desire, having the moon-crested Siva for its object, appears as far from fulfillment as ever. I do not know when that desired but unattainable person will have pity on this our friend, looked on by companions with tears, emaciated by asceticism, like Indra taking pity on ploughed ground afflicted by drought ?

Thus addressed manifestly in good will by Parvati's companion acquainted with her inmost purpose the stranger, whose signs of joy were not manifested, asked Uma thus :—" Dear lady, is this so ? or is it a joke ?"

Then depositing the wreath of crystal beds drawn inward with the fingers in the fore-parts of her hand the daughter of the mountain, her speech long suppressed, spoke in measured syllables with great difficulty.

''O thou superior adept in the Veda, as it has been heard by you, I am ambitious of getting up to high dignity. And this asceticism is but a miserable means of attaining it. But there is nothing to which a desire and hope will not resort through delusion.

The Brahmacharin said :—" Siva is known to me and you again are desirous of him. Considering him to delight in evil habits I cannot serve your purpose in such an evil choice.

O thou whose determination is set on a despicable object as Siva, how this thy hand, with the marriage string set on it, shall endure the very first encounter with Siva's hand braceletted with snakes.

Consider yourself if these two things befit each other, the bridal silk dress on which are pictures of the beatiful swan and Siva's skin-clothing showering drops of blood.

Even thy ill-wishing enemies cannot imagine such a misfortune of thine that the red-tinged steps of thy two feet set on clusters of flowers in a beautiful room will be on the cemetries with dead bodies scattered on them.

Say what can be more incongruous that Siva's embrace being easily attainable, on this thy bosom the site of yellow sandal wood the dusty ashes of funeral pyres will form a seat.

It is again a misfortune that great people seeing an old bull ridden by you, who when married, will be carried by a great elephant, will laugh and ridicule you.

By the desire of association with Siva two should be grieved for, namely, the luminous digit of the moon which is already on Siva's head and thou too equally luminous and each being the joy of the eye of this world.

His body is deformed with eyes; his birth and race are unknown; he must be extremely poor not having a rag to put on. O thou, with eyes like a deer, has he a single recommendation as bridegroom, namely the possession of beauty, wealth and dignity?

Divert your mind from such an evil desire; where such a person so low and vile and where thou who art so happy and fortunate? There is great inequality between an impaling stick at the cemetry, for execution of felons and the holy sacrificial stake consecrated by the Vedic ritual.

The Brahmin having thus spoken against her wishes she manifested anger by the quaking of her nether lips and drawing obliquely her two eyes with red corners.

She spoke to him :—Forsooth thou dost not know Siva since thou speakest thus to me. The ignorant cannot understand the character of great men which is not the same as of the world and the motives of which are incomprehensible to them.

Good things are used by persons but on remedying some evil or by one desirous of wealth and dignity. Of what use are these things by which through hope the state of mind is disturbcd to Siva who is the refuge of the universe without any desire ?

Being poor he is the source of all wealth. Roving about in cemetries he is the lord of the three worlds. Being terrific in appearance he is called Siva or felicitous. There are none that understand the essential nature of Siva.

Whether it glitters with ornaments or be endued with snakes, whether an elephant skin hangs on it or it be dressed in silk, whether it has a scull on it or the moon for its crest the body of him whose form is the universe cannot be determined.

Indra, riding on the elephant of the quarter with temporal juice distilling, touches with his crown the feet of Siva though a poor man riding a bull and makes his toe red with the pollen of full blown flowers of the celestial tree.

Even while desiring to find fault one thing has been well spoken with reference to the Lord whom the Vedas declare to be the cause even of the self-begotten Brahma. How can he be of a known origin ?

Now do away with the altercation. Let him be as has been heard by thee, so entirely and without exception. But my mind is fixed in love on him. One who acts from his own desires regards not what may be said against him.

O dear companion, this Brahmin, whose lips are quivering, is going to say something again. Don't allow him to speak for not only he who reviles a great person but he too who hears him is also a partaker of the sin.

Otherwise I shall go away from hence." Saying this the young lady was going away when Siva, whose emblem was the great bull, assuming his own form and smiling took hold of her. Seeing him, quaking, her body perspiring and taking a step the daughter of the king of mountains neither went nor stood still like a river stopped in its course by the obstruction of a mountain.

" O thou stooping in thy limbs, heneeforward I am thy slave bought by asceticisms." On the moon-crested Siva saying this she immediately forgot the exhaustion produced by austerity for fatigue becomes refreshed by success.

---

## CANTO VI.

GAURI secretly deputed her maid with a communication to Siva, the soul of the universe, saying, "The lord of the mountains is my giver, I cannot marry without his order or leave."

As the singing bird parched on the Mango branch does duty as a mouth of the tree, so the maid acted as Parvati's mouth.

Having promised "even so" and let go with difficulty Uma to her father the chastiser of Kama, called to mind the seven luminous Rishis.

Illumining the sky by their encircling lights those ascetics, having asceticism for their wealth, with Arundhuti in their company immediately arrived before the lord.

They had bathed in the streams of the etherial Ganges whose waves were throwing up the flowers of the celestial trees on the banks which were perumed with the temporal juice of the elephants of the quarters.

They wore sacrificial threads set with pearls, were clad in bark-garm ents set with gold, had rosaries of jewelled beads like desire fulfilling celestial trees and had retired from the world.

Driving his horses below and lowering his standard even the thousand-rayed sun paid obeisance to them.

At the general dissolution, they, taking hold of the earth which had been raised up, by the arms rested on the tusk of the great bear.

Because of their forming the remains of creation after Brahma sung by the archælogists they are called ancient creators.

Though enjoying the fruits of untainted asceticisms of a former birth they are still ascetics.

Being in the midst of them and her eyes cast on the feet of her husband Vasishtha, the chaste Arundhati shone much like the success of asceticism personally present.

The Lord Siva looked upon her and the Munis without distinction of dignity. That this is female and this is male is not to be regarded, the character of the good is to be honored. From seeing her Siva's desire for a wife became greater, for good wives are certainly the fundamental cause of righteous acts

For the sake of righteousness, Siva having been caused to form a regard for Parvati the mind of Kama, who was in fear for his previous transgression, again breathed in hope.

After worshipping the parent of the universe all those Munis, who could repeat all the Vedas and Vedangas with hair standing on end said.

Our prescribed study of the Veda, our offering in the fire according to rule, our practical asceticism have borne fruit to-day, since we have been made to become an object of the Spirit's mind thou having remembered and looked for us, an object which was beyond our expectation.

He is the highest of all successful persons in whose mind thou remainest, how much greater still he who remains in thy mind or in that of Brahma.

True it is we inhabit a higher station than both the sun and the moon ; but today by thy kind remembrance of us we have attained a still higher place than they.

Being honoured by thee we think highly of our-selves. Thy regard of high persons in respect of his virtues begets general credit.

That delight of ours, O thou having three eyes, which is produced from thy thinking of us cannot be related to thee who art the indwelling spirit of all embodied persons.

Thou art seen visibly but we do not know thee in thy real presence. Be favourable. Relate thyself. Thou art not within the range of natural intellects.

Is this thy form the same by which thou createst the developed universe? Or is it that by which thou preservest it? or is it the portion which destroys it? which of the three is it?

Or rather, O god, let this our high desire remain

aside. But command us who have thus presented ourselves, being thought of by thee, what we shall do.

Then the Supreme lord Siva, increasing the feeble light, by the rays of his white teeth, of the moon in his crest, replied.

As it is known to you none of my efforts is for purpose of self. By eight forms becoming thus am I not known?

I am requested to beget a son by the gods oppressed by foes as clouds are asked by Chatakas oppressed by thirst.

Therefore I wish to get Parvati for the purpose of begetting a son as the sacrificer desires to have wood or flint for the production of fire.

On my behalf you are to ask the Himalaya for her, for matrimonial alliances formed by the intervention of the good do not tend to reverses.

Having been joined in alliance with him, lofty, having stability and bearing the weight of the earth know me also not to be defrauded.

You are teachers of morals and you do not require to be taught how the Himalaya is to be addressed for his daughter.

The noble Arundhuti is also fit to render good offices in this matter; generally in such affairs there is great dexterity in matron ladies.

Therefore proceed to Oshadhiprastha (herb-peak), the capital of the Himalaya, for the accomplishment of this business. I shall expect you at this cataract of the river Mahakoshi.

On his, the chief of ascetics, becoming inclined to marriage, the ascetics, sons of Brahma, gave up their shame for having wives.

Having assented by the utterance of Om the collection of ascetics departed. The lord Siva also got to the place first pointed out.

Having got up to the sky, dark as iron, those great Rishis too, as swift as meditation, came to Oshadhiprastha.

As if Alaka (the city of Kuvera) the seat of wealth and plenty were transplanted there. Or it was built to accomodate the excess of the heavenly dwellers.

It was surrounded by Ganga's streams with herbs glittering within the ramparts and with large jewelled stone walls handsome even in its fortifications.

There elephants were stronger than lions, the horses were of the breed of Vila, one of Indra's stud, the citizens were Yakshas and Kinnaras and the women were fairies.

There the sound of drums of houses whose tops were in contact with clouds was imagined to be but the echo of the cloud's roar but was distinguished as such by the tunes.

There the beauty of flags on houses, formed without the labour of the citizens, was secured by means of celestial trees themselves with wet clothes hanging to dry on their moving branches.

At night on drinking sites of crystal palaces the reflections of celestial luminaries get the position of decorative presents of honour.

Being shown the way in inclement weather by the light of glittering herbs the rambling women do not feel that it is dark.

The inhabitants of this city were ever youthful and never fell into decrepitude. There was no other lord of death than the flower-armed god of love and no loss of sensation save the sleep after sexual intercourse.

There young men sought to propitiate the anger of women only in which their brows were contracted, their lips quaked and they threatened them with their soft fingers.

Their pleasure-garden was the fragrant Gandha-madana in which the Vidyadhara ramblers used to sleep in the shade of the celestial Samantaka trees.

Having seen the capital of the Himalaya the heavenly ascetics considered their penances in quest of heaven as useless privations.

When they alighted quickly on the mountain's house, their clotted locks, as still as painted flames, attracted the notice of the porters below.

Alighting from the sky according to seniority that row of ascetics shone like a row of suns reflected in the water.

Taking offerings and bending the earth with his heavy foot steps the mountain advanced to meet them.

With lips ruddy like red mineral, tall, having large arms like the Devadaru tree and rock-chested by nature he was at once recognized as the Himalaya.

Having paid them honours according to rule and himself the shower he introduced them into the seraglio.

The seven Rishis being seated there on seats of reed, the lord of mountains, having also taken a seat, said.

Your unexpected appearance appears like a shower without the rise of clouds or like fruits whose blossoms had never appeared.

I consider myself, by your favour, like a fool turned wise, like iron turned into gold and as if ascended to heaven from the earth.

Henceforward for the purification of creatures I shall be sought. That which has been inhabited by the adorable is called a place of pilgrimage.

I know myself to be sanctified by two things, O excellent Brahmins, by the stream of the heavenly Ganga over my head and by the washing of your feet.

I consider my body as enjoying your favour in both forms, moving about in your service and as a mountain impressed by your feet.

Though extending to the extremities of the regions my limbs cannot contain the excessive delight produced by your condescending to honor me with a visit.

By the sight of you luminaries not only is the darkness lurking in my caves dispelled, but also the greater darkness which is within myself appertaining to the quality of Rajas.

You are desireless what can I do for you. I consider your advent here to be solely for my sanctification.

Still you ought to give me a command in some little matter for servants, in respect of their lords, are favoured by appointment to some service.

Here is myself, here is my wife and this is my daughter, the life of the family; say by which of us can any thing be done for you here. I do not say any thing about gold or silver because I regard them as no substance.

Himalaya, thus speaking by means of the echo resounding from the mouths of caverns, spoke like two persons to the same effect.

Then moved by the Rishis, Angiras, the foremost in matters of speech, replied to the mountain.

All that you have offered is in your power, but greater than all this is the loftiness of thy mind which is equal to thy summits.

It is fitting that they call thee the mount Himalaya Vishnu for thy bosom has become a receptacle, like that of Vishnu himself, of all creatures moveable and immoveable.

How could the serpent have held the earth, with hoods as tender as lotus fibres if thou hast not supported it from the bottom of the lower regions.

Thy glories and thy rivers, extending uninterrupted, untainted and unrestrained by the waves of the sea, purify the worlds because of their purity.

Even as Ganga is magnified by the foot of the Supreme one, Vishnu, from which the river was produced, so also by thee, of lofty summit, its second source.

The extension of Hari's glory upward, downward and horizontally curved was at a fixed time when he took the corresponding three steps and covered all space——but thine is everlasting——thou coveredest space without any commencement.

By thee holding a place among the eaters of sacrifices the eminent golden summit of Sumeru is rendered futile.

All hardness has been made over by thee to thy fixed form but this, thy body, by which you pay honor to the good, is lowly by devotion.

Then hear the purpose of our coming. We also share in the labour, O mountain king, since we carry to thee the message. He who holds, with the half moon, the high title of Ishwara endowed with the eight attributes, which is not shared by any other person, by whom this universe is held by his eight forms calculated to assist one another by their respective powers as a carriage is held on the road by horses, whom situated with the body the yogis seeks, whose site is free from the fear of revolving, he Sambhu, the observer of the world's doings, himself the giver of boons, asks for thy daughter through us.

Thou art fit to unite him as the sense with thy daughter as the word, for a daughter given to a good husband is not to be regretted by the father. Let all the creatures, fixed and moveable, turn Uma into their mother for the Lord Siva is the father of the universe.

Let the gods, having bowed to the blue necked, illumine her two feet with the light of their crest jems.

Uma is the bride, you are the giver, ourselves the petitioners for Siva and Sambhu is the bride-groom. Indeed this ceremonial is sufficient for the exaltation of thy race.

By means of alliance through thy daughter you become the father-in-law of the father of the universe who is a lauder of none, but is lauded, who is adored by all, but himself adores none.

The divine ascetic thus speaking Parvati, remaining by her father's side with the head downwards, was counting the petals of her lotus.

Although fully desirous the mountain looked up to the face of Mena for advice. In matters concerning daughters generally the heads of families follow the leading of wives.

Mena too assented to the desired business of her

husband. Chaste and devoted wives never oppose the wishes of their husband.

Having considered well the proposal and given a well-thought-out reply to the Rishi the mountain took hold of her daughter auspiciously and said—

"Come, O chlld, thou art destined an alms-giving to the soul of the universe. The sages are themselves the petitioners and the fruit of married life is obtained by me."

Having thus addressed his daughter the mountain spoke to the ascetics :—"Parvati bows to you all as the bride of the three-eyed Siva."

Having cheered the speech of the mountain which became important by the accomplishment of their desired object, they magnified Ambica by benedictions whose fruition was at hand.

Arundhati took her up in her arms whose two golden ear-rings dropped off by her eagerness to make a bow and blushing.

Arundhati also removed the grief of her mother whose face was full of tears at the prospect of parting with her daughter and who was overcome by her affection to her daughter by relating the virtues of the bride-groom who had no other consort before.

Having been asked by Siva's future relation for an auspicious wedding day the bark-clothed Munis fixed one after three days and went away.

Bidding good bye to Himalaya, meeting Siva

again and communicating to him the success of their business, they dismissed by him went up to the sky.

Impatiently anxious for the company of the mount's daughter, the lord of brutes, too, Siva passed three days with difficulty. Why would not love disturb other weak creatures, subject to the senses, since it touches even the master of his senses.

---

## CANTO VII.

In the light fortnight and on the day endowed with the virtues of the auspicious Jamitra (the seventh) the Himalaya, with his relations, celebrated the scarament of matrimony of his daughter.

By the celebration of ceremonial festivities for matrimony from house to house in consequence of the people's regard the whole city of the mountain in which the matrons were eagerly engaged as well as seraglio resembled one large household.

That city, with its high-ways strewn with flowers of heavenly trees, with its waving flags made of China silken cloth, by the brilliance of gate ways of shining gold, shone like a second heaven.

Though there were other sons and daughters Uma, because her hand was about to be received by a bride-groom, became peculiarly dear as life of her parents as if she was an only child as if she were found after being lost and as if she had been dead and had risen again.

Having benedictions pronounced on her she went from bosom to bosom and every relative presented her jewels. The affection of the mountain's race though shared by other relatives was now centred in in her as its one repositary.

At the sacred hour to Mitra, the asterism posterior Phalguni having got in*o conjunction with the moon, the female relatives, who had husbands and sons living, made decorations on her body.

She was adorned with *durva* grass sprouts mixed with white mustard seeds. The decoration of the annointment was beautiful all through. She was clad in a silken raiment reaching up to the middle and furnished with an arrow according to the Kshatrya custom.

The girl, having got possession of a new sacramental arrow, shone like the lunar curve, at the close of the dark fortnight increasing by the rays of the sun.

The women conducted her, the oil on whose body was absorbed by *lodhra* powders, whose body had been coloured by a dry yellow fragrant drug and who was clothed in a raiment adapted to the ablution, towards the quadrangular bath room.

In that room paved with emerald stones, beautified with rows of pearls set in it they bathed her with water from golden pots inclined to pour their contents amid the sound of trumpets.

Parvati, being purified in the body by the holy ceremonial bath and being clothed in fresh clothing for meeting the bride-groom, shone like the earth supplied with a good water-wash from thunder-clouds.

She was then conducted by women devoted to their husbands from the bathing place to the middle of the auspicious altar on which was prepared a seat with canopy over it and joined with four pillars of jems.

Having set there the slender one with her face towards the east the women tarried for a moment, their eyes attracted by her natural beauty though the articles of decoration were near.

A woman tied the extremety of her hair, which had been dried by the heat of incense, with flowers in it, as a fine knot, by means of a wreath of the yellow Madhuka intermingled with Durva grass.

They decorated her body, already perfumed with Aguru perfume, with saffron paint. She stood there excelling the beauty of the three-streamed Ganga whose sand banks were set off by the yellow Chakravakas.

Having excelled in beauty the lotus with black bees sticking to it and the moon's disc with streaks of clouds about it her beauty, by means of her decorated tresses, abolished the use of their names as exemplars of beauty.

On account of the acquisition of excellency of color, the stalk of barley, which was placed on her ears, fixed the eyes of spectators on her checks, whitened by the application of Lodhra powders and rendered excessively orient by the application of saffron.

The fruition of Parvati's beauty, who had a body symmetrical in its parts, whose under-lip was marked by a line the redness of which was refined by a little wax, was near at hand.

Having been blessed by a maid jocosely after being decorated by the same maid in her feet with red dyes saying "touch the lunar digit on thy husband's head with this thy foot", she, as a return for such a blessing, struck her silently with a flower wreath.

The black dye was applied to her two eyes, beautiful as a full blown lotus, not from an idea of its increasing the beauty of the eye but because it was auspicious as a protection from evil influences.

On being endued with ornaments she shone like a creeper by means of flowers springing up, like the night by means of rising luminaries and like a river by means of birds adhering to its banks.

And having looked at, in the reflection of a mirror, her beautiful body with her large eyes she became eager for the reception of Hara for the decoration of women has for its fruit the oservance of their husbands.

Having taken with two fingers yellow orpiment and red arsenic, as an auspicious mixture dye, and having raised her head, on the two ears of which were attached two splendid ear-rings, her mother,

Mena, being over come with tears of joy, performed with difficulty *tilaka* of her daughter's matrimonial ceremony, in whose mind after the commencement of youth, a strong desire had taken place for the first time.

With eyes agitated by tears she also tied the auspicious matrimonial arm-band of wool on Uma's hand also as an amulet which was, by her agitation, fixed to a wrong place but which was set right by the nurse's fingers.

Clad in fresh silk or linen and holding a new mirror she repeatedly shone like the shore of the milk-ocean streaken with foam flakes, and an autumnal night with full moon.

Knowing what ceremonies were necessary the mother assisted her, the perpetuator of the family, to make obeisance to the adorable family-gods and made her touch the feet of the chaste women according to grades.

Uma, bowing down, was addressed by them, " Acquire the undivided love of thy husband." But she having possession of half his body her happiness, on marrying Siva, exceeded their best wishes.

Having completed the initial ceremony of her marriage with a magnificence equal to his wishes, his joyous interest and wealth, the happy mountain, himself courteous, remained in the assembly of his relations expecting the advent of the bull-sigued Siva.

Meanwhile on Kailasha ornaments corresponding to the former marriage ornaments were placed in front of Siva, the chastiser of the city Tripura by the seven regardful divine mothers.

Out of reverence for them the Beauty of those auspicious ornaments was only touched by the Lord Siva who himself underwent an alteration suitable for a wedding.

The ashes did duty for scented ointment, the skulls, which Siva carried about him, put forth the beauty of the pure crest jem and on the borders of the elephant hide itself became the appearance of silken dress with pictures of swans.

The third eye, which was shining in the middle of the frontal bone within which was situated a pure twany pupil, served the purpose of the yellow arsenic painting on the fore-heed.

The snakes disappeared as such but their jems did duty for ornaments of Siva's body.

Siva having the moon for his crest jem required no other ornament for his head.

Thus the only generative cause of miracles, Siva, the creator of perfect decoration by his own power, looked at himself attached to the reflection in the sword blade brought by the troops near him.

Leaning on Nandi's arm and mounted on his great bull whose large back was covered by a tiger skin and which through reverence for him had contracted his huge stature like Mount Kailasha, he set out for his marriage procession.

Following him, the seven divine mothers, whose ear-rings were waving by the shaking of their vehicles, turned the sky like unto a reservoir of lotuses reddened by the dust of their haloes of splendour.

And after them whose splendour was that of gold appeared the goddess Kali ornamented with skulls like a range of black clouds attended by cranes and casting lightings far in front.

Then the sound of the auspicious trumpet caused by the troops of Siva, going in advance, declared to the goods the oppurtunity of worshipping Siva.

The sun of a thousand rays held his umbrella made fresh by the divine artist Vishwakarma. Having his head not far from its silk Siva appeared as one on whose head the Ganges was falling.

Though in form different from rivers yet recognised as it were by being accompanied by flights of swans, Ganga and Jamuna too, in embodied forms, served the god with chowries.

Magnifying his glory by the expressions "Prosper like fire magnified by clarified butter" the first creator Brahma and Vishnu, the soul, bearing the mystic mark of Srivatsa, came to him.

The one only form was divided three fold. Sometimes Hara or Siva was senior to Vishnu and Hari or Vishnu to him and Brahma to both; and they too Vishnu and Siva were sometimes prior to Brahma.

Humbly attired by laying aside their parapharnalia of state Indra and other divine rulers of several worlds applied to Nandi for introduction to Siva's presence. And being presented by him they prostrated themselves with joined palms.

Siva returned the complements to Brahma by a nod, to Hari by conversation, to Indra, the killer of Vitra, by a smile, and to all other gods by the sight itself according to seniority.

The seven Rishis blessed him saying "Prosper" and he spoke to them with a smile:—"In the matrimonial sacrifice here celebrated you have been chosen by me as priests."

Saying it Siva, who had a lunar digit in his crest, went on whose exploits at Tripura were being sung by expert Gandharvas with Viswavasu as their leader, himself being perfectly dispassionate.

The bull going beautifully with golden bells resounding, constantly shaking his two horns, and dipped in the clouds as from strokes on the surface when fixed in the mind, carried him in the sky.

The bull reached in a moment the city which had never encountered an enemy's attack and defended by the chief of mountains, being drawn in by the rays shot from his eyes as by strings of gold.

Being looked at by the citizens with upward faces from curiosity and having descended from the etherial way marked by his own arrows when discharged against Tripura Siva, whose throat was cloud black, reached the vicinity of the earth's surface.

Pleased at 'Siva's coming, the emperor of the mountains advanced to recieve him with troops of elephants mounted on by relations, having rich ornaments as with his own mountain sides with trees rich with flowers.

On the gates of the city door being opened two companies of the followers of the god and the mountain went together whose clangor went a long way like two streams breaking through the same sluice gate.

The mountain shrank on being bowed to by Hara adored by the three worlds for he did not notice that his own head at first had been lowly bent by Siva's majesty.

Going before his future son-in-law the Himalaya, the splendour of his face glowing with joy, made him enter his wealthy city in which flowers were strewn ankle deep in the ways of the shops.

Giving up all other business the beauteous females of the city tried in rows of palaces only to look at Ishana.

Suddenly starting up to the lattices one female will not stay to bind her long black tresses dropping down save by the hand.

Another took her foot away from her maiden on which the dye was wet and streaming and rushed in haste to the chamber. And wherever she went she impressed it with a crimson foot-print.

Another having adorned the right eye with collyrium the left eye still destitute of that decoration went hurriedly to the window with pencil in the hand.

The waist band, of another female, rising up in haste, half stringed with diamonds and therefore dropping them at every step, had at that time the string as the residuum sticking to the tip of the great toe.

The bull-eyed windows, their holes filled with the faces in which was the perfume of wines and in which the rolling eyes of the ladies excited deeply by curiosity were like flying black bees, were ornamented as it were by lotuses.

Then the moon-crested Siva passed into the high road abounding in flags and high gate-ways, making the domes of palaces even in the day doubly splendid by the effusion of moon-light from his crest.

The women were so absorbed in the sight of Siva that they did not notice any thing else for the functions of their other senses had, as it were by universal identity, all entered the eye.

Rightly did Uma, though so tender, practise such difficult asceticism for such a husband. Most fortunate are the women who may obtain even the state of a slave to him, what then must be said of her who obtains repose on his bosom.

If the creator had not united this conple of a beauty to be coveted by all surely the labour of his creating such a beauty would have been fruitless.

Forsooth the body of the flower-bannered Kama was not burnt by Siva possessed by wrath. I think on seeing this god Kama, of his own accord, gave up his body from shame.

Having obtained alliance with this lord, O fortunate, which had long been the desire of his heart, the king of mountains, shall hold, O dear companion, his head already lofty from his supporting the earth, still higher.

Thus hearing the words, of the women of Oshadhiprastha pleasing to the ear the three-eyed Siva came into the abode of the Himalya where handfuls of parched grain were in their downward course by the bracelets of the crowded women.

Siva leaning on Vishnu's arm, having alighted there like the sun, from his Bull white like the autumnal cloud, entered the other courtyard of the lord of mountains which had been entered before by the lotus-seated Brahma.

Following him, the gods too with Indra as their leader and the great Rishis with the seven Rishis as their leaders and his hosts came to the abode of the mountain like the most excellent objects coming after unfailing undertakings.

Having got a seat the lord Siva fittingly accepted the offering of honor with jems, and curds with honey or wine and a pair of new silk dresses all presented by the mountain the mantras not being neglected.

Clad in silk he was next conducted near to the bride by respectful persons familiar with the seraglio, as the sea, with its line of froth manifest, is led near to the coast by the new lunar rays.

The appearance of Uma elated the heart of Siva just as the moon does the water lily kumuda, and then Siva's heart became as cheerful as the waters are by the full blown Kumuda, as the whole world is by the autumn with its clear moon.

Becoming unstable on their encountering each other the eyes of the two were a litttle fixed for the ceremonious exchange of looks. Then turning back and coveting each other they felt the torment of shame.

The eight-formed Siva took hold of her hand with red fingers presented by the chief of mountains as the first shoot of Kama, who, afraid of him, had concealed his body in that of Uma.

Uma's horripilation manifested itself and the bull-signed Siva too became perspiring in the fingers. By the joining of their hands the operation of Kama was as it were equally divided.

Other ordinary couples, whose reception of hands is brought about, sustain first rate beauty by the vicinity of these two. How is to be described then the beauty of that couple?

By their going round and keeping on the right a fire blazing upward that couple shone like the day and night revolving at the lateral extremities of the mount Meru, joined together.

Having conducted that couple with closed eyes by contact with each other, thrice around the fire the priest caused the bride to cast the parched grain in that blazing flame.

Under the priest's instruction the bride brought doubled palm-fuls of the parched grain smoke of an agreeable scent to her facc, which was spiring over the cheeks and serving for the time as the ear-lotus for her.

By the reception of the ritual smoke the bride's face, whose ear ornamens of barley were withered, became a little moist and ruddy on the cheeks tinged with the black collyrium issuing out of the two eyes.

The priest said to the bride:—" O child, this fire is witness to the fact of your marriage with Siva. Abandoning controversy you should pay implicit obedience to your husband."

That saying of the priest having entered into the ears to the extremety of the eyes was recieved into the inmost mind by Bhavani as the first rain is drunk by the earth excessively heated in the summer season.

Having been directed by the everlasting one the husband, lovely to behold, to look at the polar star, she, having lifted her face and growing nervous, said with difficulty " it has been looked at."

Having been made to go through the ceremony of marriage by the priest learned in the ritual, these two, the parents of all creatures, bowed to Brahma sitting on the lotus seat.

The bride was saluted on return by the Creator with the benedictory words :—" O beauteous one, be thou a mother of heroes." Though eloquent he could not say anything to Siva for what could possibly be an object of desire to him?

Afterwards having come to a quandrangular altar strewn with ritual substances and sitting on golden seats the husband and wife experienced the sprinkling of moist grain customary among people and therefore not to be disregarded.

The goddess Lakshmi held on them a lotus umbrella having a large lotus stalk stick which had got the splendour of strings of pearls by means of multitudes of water-drops adhering to the extremities of leaves.

By a language uttered in a two-fold manner, Sanskrit and Prakrita the goddess Saraswati praised the husband in Sanskrit and the bride in Prakrit which was easily comprehensible.

They saw for a while the first scene of the Apsaras in which varying actions were manifested according to the five different articulation, in which different modes were set answering the different sentie ments of love, satire, pity and in which were exhibited their graceful gestures.

Afterwards having prostrated themselves with doubled palms on their crests the gods asked of Hara who has just married a wife to accept some service from the five arrowed Kama who at the termination of the curse had resumed his form.

Free from anger the lord now permitted in himself even the operation of his arrows. Certainly a representation made in the proper season by men conversant with business, to their lords, becomes sucessful.

Having dismissed the gods and taking the daughter of the mountain by the hand the moon-crested Siva came to the sleeping house having golden pots full of water endued with the beauty of flowery decoration and on the floor of which were spread beddings.

There the lord made Gauri laugh secretly by the funny actions of his follower's faces. Gauri, who was ornamented with the modest shame of a recent marriage, drew her face lifted by him and spoke with difficulty even to maids that used to sleep with her.

---

## CANTO VIII.

**After** Siva's marriage with the daughter of the mountain-chief she was afraid of having a free sexual intercourse with him, still his desire was satisfied. In the beginning the daughter of the mountain used to give no reply to the words of Mahadeva. On his holding her cloth she wished to free herself and go away and used to lie with her face against him still the newly-wedded Parvati conduced to his satisfaction.

When the Lord out of curiosity used to close his eye-lids as if in sleep Parvati used confidently to fix her eyes on him. Afterwards smiling a little he used to open his eyes and she, as if struck by a lightning, used to close her own.

When her beloved consort used to place his hands on her navel she used to obstruct him but the cloth round her waist used to be loosened of itself. Her friends used to instruct Parvati saying "friend, without the least fear, satisfy Sankara secretly." But when she used to come before her beloved she forgot every thing. When Shankara used to vouchsafe proposals of intercourse Parvati used to accept them by her looks and to reply by the shaking of her head.

When in a solitary place Sankara used to take away her raiment Parvati used to shut up his eyes with her hands. But she found no means to obstruct the vision of the eye situate on his forehead, and so all her efforts were futile.

She used to take away her lips when kissed by him and her hands used to give way when embraced ruthlessly. Although the husband is pained at heart still rare is the attempt of the newly married brides to prevent the delightful endeavour of the husbands to hold sexual intercourse.

None else but Parvati could bear the intercourse of Siva in which he used to kiss her without cutting her lips and place his nails (on the breast) without wounding her. When her friends used to press her to describe the incidents of the night she could not do so out of shame.

When taking up a mirror Parvati used to mark the signs of intercourse her beloved consort used to go stealthily behind her back. Seeing the reflection of her beloved behind her own, she used to feel abashed and exclaim " What is this ? What is this ?"

Seeing that Mahadeva was enjoying the youthfulness of Parvati her mother was exceedingly happy; when daughter becomes a favourite of her hausband the mother feels no other misery. Maheshwara having spent thus a few days in her company Parvati gradually perceived the pleasure of sexual intercourse and felt no more any pain in conseqnence thereof. Then she used to return the embrace of her husband, and did not take away her face when solicited for a kiss. And when her husband used to] hold the ornament on her waist she used to hold his hands lightly. Within a short time from gestures it could be perceived, that they were mutually] attached to each other. They used to flatter each other and feel pangs even for a short separation. The wife used to please her husband in the same way as the latter used to do the former. As the river Janhavi does not go elsewhere leaving the ocean and the ocean too does not go anywhere leaving her so their love prospered without experiencing the least separation.

Maheshwara instructed Parvati secretly in the art of sexual intercourse and made her a disciple. She, too learning that dexterous art of youthful women, made a *Dakshina* (preceptor's present) of all delightful contrivances of intercourse.

When she used to feel pain on accouut of her love biting her lips she used to move about her fingers, and afterwards when let loose she used to remove the pain by the cool rays of the moon. When Shankara's eye on the forehead was besmeared with the scented powders from Parvati's tresses at the time of kissing he used to clear it up by the lotus scented wind of her mouth. Thus engaged in sexual intercourse and showing 'favour towards Manmatha, Shankara spent a month in Uma's company, at the residence of the Mountain-chief.

Then with the permission of the Himalaya and Menaka stricken with grief consequent upon the separation from their daughter, Shankara, being within his own self, riding his own bull of unmitigated course, roamed at large happily.

Having placed Uma first on that bull, swift as the wind, the Lord Shankara sat behind her and therefore taking before Uma's rising breasts he came to the mount Sumeru. And there making a house of golden creepers he enjoyed the pleasure of pressing the breasts and sexual intercourse. He lived a few days on the mount Mandara resorted to, by the black-bee, drinking the honey of Parvati's lotus-face, and made of rocks impressed with the foot-prints of the lotus-navelled deity.

The Lord of mountains and the preceptor of the universe went to a twane-coloured mountain. There terrified at the terrific roars of the elephants Parvati threw her tender arms around his neck. And removing her anxiety he enjoyed beautiful moon-light there. Once on a time he went to the mount Malaya and enjoyed sexual intercourse with his wife. Shaking the sandal forest and carrying the filaments of Lavanga creepers, light southern wind removed the exhaustion of his wife consequent upon the sexual intercourse. There while bathing in a stream, Parvati, finding fault with her husband, struck him with a golden lily. Mahadeva took up water in his palms and threw it at Parvati's eyes which, thereat, were immediately closed. While thus sporting Sapharis moved about Uma's waist and her tongue appeared two-fold in the water. Thereupon they repaired to the garden of Nandana where he performed her decoration with Sachi's favourite Parijata flowers and was seen by Apsaras.

Thus did enjoy Shankara heavenly and earthly joy in Parvati's company. Afterwards when the sun's rays became very fierce they repaired to the mount Gandhamadana. There seated on a golden rock and seeing the Sun, capable of being seen, the Lord said to his wife, reclining on his left arm.

"Dear! look, the Sun, applying the beauty of the lotus to its two extremeties, bright like your eyes, is destroying the day like the lord of subjects destroying the universe at the final dissolution. Behold, the sun declining, the fountains, of your father, deprived of its rays, have been divorced from the rain-bows. Having feasted on the filaments of lotus in the lake the pair of Chakravas have left each other's neck and are being painfully separated from eaeh other. Having left their sweet scented habitations of the day the elephants are going to live in the water abounding in black bees living inside the closed lotuses. Look, O dear, the sun, by his long reflection. in the west, has made a golden bridge in the lake. Having spent the day in the lake the leaders of the boar-herd are coming out with lily stalks in their tusks. See, O thou having pointed breasts, the peococks, waiting under trees and spreading a circle of white are as if drinking the declining sun. Darkness appearing in the east, a portion of the sky, the water of which being drunk up by the sun, is looking like a lake full of lotuses almost dried up. Look, O dear, the deer are entering into hermitages; the trees, with their roots well watered, are appearing beautiful with growing leaves. The sacrificial cows are entering into hermitages, and the sacrificial fire of the evening is being lighted up. By these the hermitages have put on a most beautiful ap earance.

The lotuses out of love have not been closed as yet so that the black-bees may soon occupy their residences. By the sun of limited rays the western quarter is appearing like a maiden decorated with Bandhujiva flowers. Reciting the Sama Vedas in a sweet voice thousands of Rishis, living on the sun's rays, are chanting the glories of the sun transfering its own heat to the fire. Having placed the day within the great ocean, the lord of the day is setting with his horses, with their manes down. The setting of the sun illustrates a great truth, *viz.*, the greater rises a luminous body the more is its depression at the time of the setting. Though the feet of the sun followed the twilight, his heat was deposited in the setting hill for why would not he, whom he had rewarded at the time of rising, follow him in this hour of danger?

Look, O thou of curling locks, how crimson, yellow and red clouds are looking beautiful. Perhaps the evening has decoratted them so that you will see them. Look the mountain is dividing the evening heat amongst the manes of the lions, creeper-producing trees and its summits covered with minerals. Look, O dear, the ascetics, conversant with rituals, rising up from the earth are making oblations of sacred water, and after performing all the evening rites they are reciting the sweet Vedic mantras. O thou of sweet speech, the time for my evening rites has also come. Permit me therefore to perform them. These thy companious, of the same age with thee, will please you.

Thereupon showing disregard at the words of her husband by the gesture of her lips Parvati began to converse with Vijaya who was near her. Even the Iswara himself went to perform the evening rites by reciting mantras. Beholding that Parvati did not reply to him out of jealousy Maheswara again appeared before her and smiling a little said " Useless is thy wrath, O Parvati, cast it off therefore. I have been governed by Sandhya and not by any other female. I enjoy thy company always—the only separation is in the evening for performing Sandhya rites. Our union is like that of the pair of Chakravakas. Do you not know it? O thou of beautiful limbs! O sensitive lady, the body which was cast off by the sensitive lady, the body, which was cast off by the self-sprung after creating the progenitors, is serving the rising and setting. For that reason I attach so much importance to this matter. For that reason like unto the well-fixed earth she is assailed by darkness. Look how she appears beautiful like a river issuing out of molten minerals with forests of Tamala on one of its banks. With the red circular disc of the sun in the evening rising obliquely the western quarter has assumed crimson hue like a field of battle.

O thou of large-eyes, when the light, begotten by the union of day and night, will be possessed by Sumeru all the ten quarters will be enveloped by pitch darkness. In the night vision proceeds no where, up, down, behind and before. The universe lies in darkness like an embryo in the womb. Look O dear, darkness is putting all on the same level, pure or impure, fixed or moveable, straight or curve. The distinction between the good and evil has been done away with. Oh! fie on darkness. O thou having a lotus face, forsooth the moon is rising for destroying the darkness of the night. Look the quarters appear to have been covered with the filaments of Ketaka flowers. Hiding himself behind the Mandara mountain the moon is seeing the night full of stars. O dear, you have come to me with your companions. He has appeared behind us as if to hear what conversation passes between us.

The moon-like smiles of the formerly-seen body were kept obscured from view, but urged by the night the quarters are throwing them out like a deep secret. As if displaying water by means of the rays of the moon like Pryangu flowers, the sky is troubling the pair of Chakravakas. The moon has appeared for furnishing you with ear-ornaments. You can with yours nails, pointed as needless, cut off the new barley stalks. Holding the darkness like tresses with finger-like rays the moon is kissing the closed lotus like face of the night.

O Parvati, the rays of the newly risen sun piercing the thick darkness of the sky it is looking like the Manasa lake spoiled by the elephants. Having cast off his crimson hue the moon assumed a circular form of pure white; occasional defects of persons, who are by nature pure, are never permanent. By the water trickling from moon jems, watered by the rays of the moon the mountains are awaking in proper time the peacocks sleeping on their waist. O thou of unblemished beauty, spreading his rays on the top of desire-fulfilling trees, the moon is as if coming to count their gifts. According to the height and depression of the mountain, this moon-light, accompanied with darkness, is appearing like a painting painted on the bodies of the elephants inebriated with the trickling of temporal juice. As if being unable to bear this yellow light of the moon's rays, the lilies, devoid of the humming of black-bees, are unfolding themselves quickly.

O Chandi, the wind blowing, the cloth, tied to the desire-fulfilling tree, bathed with the pure rays, but shaken by the wind, is appearing as fickle. With the drops of the lunar rays, tender like flowers dropped at the foot of a tree, and sticking on the leaves taken up by fingers, your tresses may be beautifully decorated. As the newly married bride, trembling in fear to approach her husband, is united with him in proper time so the stars, of feeble light, are being united with the moon.

O thou having eyes in which lunar rays are settled, pure lunar rays are as if coming out from thy cheeks, which are pale white by digestion, mill-white like Shara reeds & delighted by the delightful Nature.

The presiding Goddess of this mount Gandhamadana, has brought for you the honey of celestial tree in a crimson-coloured vessel made of moonstone.

Your mouth is by nature sweet-scented by raw ilaments ; your eyes are by nature dark ; if wine is placed here can it change the natural quality? or let your companions, ever respectful and devoted to you, drink this wine which excites sexual desire.

Saying these noble words Mahadeva caused Ambika to drink the wine. Parvati felt sweet intoxication. She then followed him like a person humbled by unquestionable laws. Then with growing desire, devoid of shame and anxious to go to bed, the beautiful-faced Parvati placed herself between wine and Mahadeva.

Then Iswara began to drink, not by his mouth, but by his eyes, the face of Parvati, furnished with rolling eyes, faltering speech, drops of perspiration and sweet smile in consequence of intoxication. Then carrying Parvati, with hanging golden Mekhala, heavy on account of her heavy waist Siva entered the room of Manistones, covered with ashes, constructed for his meditation.

As the moon lies down on the autumnal clouds so Siva too, with his dear wife, laid himself down on a bed beautiful like the banks of the Ganges and spread with a cover white like a swan. There he held sexual intercourse with Parvati, in which her locks were scattered, sandal pastes were dissipated, cuts were made on her person with nails and her waist band was torn. Still Shankara was not satiated with Parvati. When the luminious bodies began to decline she pressed Mahadeva on her breast and closed her eyes sportively. After the termination of the night Kinnaras began to sing benedietory songs by playing Murchana on their respective flutes. Parvati then aroused him and he opened his eyes along with the Sun. Then they released themselves from each other's embrace. The wind coming from the forest skirt of the mount Gandhamadana, which creates waves in the Manasa lake, began to serve them.

Mahadeva was then marking the marks of nails on Parvati's thighs. She began to draw her loosened cloth but Mahadeva prevented her. Parvati's eys were reddened with night-keeping; her lips were cut deeply; her paint on the forehead was washed off and her tresses were scattered. Mahadeva lost himself on seeing Parvati's countenance.

Light set in after the termination of the night. Still Maheshwara could not leave the bed the cover of which was raised some where and depressed elsewhere, on which the Mekhala was heaped, and which was tinged with the dye of the foot.

Shankara began to drink day and night the nectar of his dear's mouth capable of enhancing his delight. When any visitor used to come Vijaya brought the news to him and he recieved him.

As the fire inside the ocean is not satiated with drinking its water so Shambhu, enjoying in the company of Parvati, spent a hundred seasons like one night. Still his desire for sexual enjoyment was not satiated.

---

## CANTO IX.

ONCE while entering the house of pleasure, Shankara, the black-bee of the lotus face of his dear consort and ever engaged in conversation of love, saw a pigeon speaking on love. That pigeon was swelling his throat and rolling his red eyes and moving his tail. His wings were set disorderly and he was showing signs of joy caused by inward lust. His fore feet were covered with small feathers and white. He was moving about in circles. Beholding that peacock coming out like a messenger of foam from the lake of nectar where Rati and Manmatha were sporting the moon-crested Siva experienced delight for a short time.

Beholding that beautiful celestial pigeon and understanding that he was Agni under the guise of a bird, he, in anger, with his eye-brows contracted, appeared dreadful.

Thereupon trembling in fear the fire, with clasped hands, said to the destroyer of Cupid.

"O lord, thou art the only lord of the universe, and dost destroy the dangers of the dwellers of heaven. O lord of asceticism, assailed by the Daityas, Indra and other deities are adoring thee. Enjoying thy dear wife's love thou hast spent a hundred seasons. Thou art living in a solitary place. And therefore not being able to see thee the celestials and their lord have been overpowered with misfortune. O thou Omniscient! Solicited by the Devas, waiting for an opportunity to serve thee, I, assuming the form of a bird have come here in search of thee. Thus, O lord, thinking all this in thy mind, do thou pardon us. All the celestials seek refuge with thee. We have been defeated by our enemies and cannot bear any more delay. O lord, be propitiated and and procreate a son. Making him his General, the king of gods may regain the prosperity of heaven and govern the three worlds by thy favour."

Hearing that sensible prayer of fire Shankara was pleased and the dwellers of mountains propitiated him with many panegyric verses.

Shankara, the destroyer of Madana, ever pleased at heart began to think of creating the destroyer of Taraka and the success of Indra's General.

Then the sexual intercourse of Mahadeva, who

could control the discharge of seminal fluid, being obstructed, he began to discharge the same fluid unbearable like the fire of dissolution. He threw it into fire of golden semen. The unbearable semen of the destroyer of Smara being thrown into him the mirror-like, pure body of fire, all on a sudden spoiled by steam and air, assumed a disfigured hue. The pleasure of her sexual intercourse being obstructed the daughter of the mountain imprecated angrily a terrible curse on fire.

"Highly wicked is your action. Therefore you will eat every thing, be visited by leprosy and other diseases and there will be smoke in your womb." Like the moon visited by consumption on account of Daksha's imprecation, like a lotus petal disfiguired by frost the fire, assuming a disfigured body, departed.

Beholding fire in that plight Maheshwara, with various sweet words relating to the art of sexual intercourse, began to enliven the mind of the daughter of the mountain, who was smiling a little out of shame and whose mind was humbled.

With the corner of his cloth Mahadeva rubbed the mark of collyrium extended by the incessant drops of perspiration on the stain-less and moon-like countenance, of his dear wife. With his trembling hand, with fingers perspiring he gently rubbed the perspiration of the lotus-like countenance of Parvati and fanning her he soon made her comfortable.

The moon-crested Siva tied with garlands of Parijata flowers the tresses of Parvati unloosened and fallen on her with flowers dropping on account of her enjoying with him. The moon-faced destroyer of Smara painted Parvati's palm with musk as if writing the world enchanting letters of Smara there. Thereupon Mahadeva put *Tathanka* on her which became as it were the wheels of the car of the flower-bannered Kama desirous of conquering the world, by which he would get on his car, her face, and conquer the world. He put a necklace of pearls around her neck spreading on her breasts. It looked like two streams of the Ganges on the summit of the mount Sumeru.

The destroyer of Smara decorated, with Rasana garlands, the waist of Parvati bearing in rows marks of nails. It appeared like the noose of Manmatha for binding his deer-like mind. Making collyrium in the fire on his fore-head he put it into her eyes like two new lotuses. Embraced by her in delight he rubbed his finger on his own blue throat. Shankara put red dye on the tip of the lotus foot of that lotus-eyed goddess and then washed off his hand with the water of the Ganges on his head. Then rubbing the mirror against his own body covered with ashes and cleansing it thereby he held it before his wife, dear as his life, so that she might mark the beauty of decoration. Seeing the marks of sexunl intercourse on her own body reflected in the mirror held up by her dear husband she felt herself abashed. Her deep attachment manifested itself in the shape of the stirring of hairs.

Casting off shame and looking in the mirror with a little smile at the decoration made by her husband Parvati considered herself the foremost of all lucky women.

In the meantime, her beloved companions Jaya and Vijaya intervening began to serve Parvati lying at a distance from the moon-crested Siva. Then the Vaitalikas began to sing auspicious songs outside on the beautifully painted altar. For pleasing the trident-handed deity the Gandharvas began to sing in accompaniment with the blowing of conchs.

Then at the time proper for the deities to look upon Mahadeva Nandi came there and bowing with folded hands communicated to him their desire for service.

Holding the daughter of the mountain by the hand, after sexual intercourse and moving slowly like swans in the lake of Manasa Siva set out towards the celestials.

Thereupon Indra and other Gods, in order, came and bowed with placing their hands on their heads unto Maheswara and the Himalaya's daughter Uma, the mother of the three worlds.

Having welcomed and dismissed the gods the bull-signed deity, leaning on Nandi's arms, got upon his bull and went away with Parvati. Then going by the ethereal way on his bull, quick-coursing like the mind he began to enjoy the breeze accompanied with the smell of Parijata flowers grown on the mountain.

Thereupon the trident-handed Siva arrived at the crystal mountain Kailasha, touching the sky, holding cresent and containing serpents and riches.

Their husbands bowing to them, the sensitive Siddha damsels, seeing their reflection on the crystal, look towards others by mistake. The marks of the moon reflected on the crystal and beautified by its lustre, display beauty at musk-deer set to play by Gouri. Seeing the reflection of their own forms on the crystal and mistaking them for other elephants, the chiefs of the herds strike them fiercely with their tusks and move about with wounds on their faces and tusks.

Seeing the reflection of stars in night on crystal palaces the Siddha damsels are about to catch them mistaking them for pearls dropped at the time of sexul intercourse. The sky-ranging, mirror-like moon is ranging on the summit as the abode of Siva and the price-less crest jem of the mountain-chief. The celestials, assailed by Cupid, meeting their loves in secret, display their forms as many, although one, on being reflected on the crystal.

On the summit of the crystal mountain the moon-crested Siva spent many days, in sportive amusement in Gouris' company. Holding the hand of the destroyer of Smara, the charmingly sportive Gouri went in ways making a beautiful sound, instructed by Nandi preceding with a cane in hand.

Hinted by Mahadeva by the contraction of his eye-brows Bhringi began to dance, by moving his horns and making various hideous gestures, for pleasing Parvati. Commanded by his own lord the Maheshawara in delight Kali, for pleasing Siva's consort, began to dance shaking the garlands of skulls around his neck and making various gestures with his hideous teeth. When Bhringi and Kali thus danced hideously, the damsel, stricken with fear and losing all control over her limbs, sat on Mahadeva's lap and embraced him fiercely. When Parvati, with her rising breasts, pressed him in embrace Maheshwara was filled with unknown delight and worked up with desire. Thus pleased by the daughter of the mountain by various means the moon-crested Siva lived happily on the mount Kailasa with his own followers,

---

## CANTO X.

Thereupon carrying that fierce and great energy of Maheshwara the fire arrived at the court of the king of celestials encircled by the gods. Then Indra, the king of gods, looked respectfully with his thousand eyes at the fire, incapable of being seen, with a smoke-coloured burning circle, Seeing Agni in that plight Indra thought for a long time that he might have caused anger to the enemy of Kandarpa. Seeing Agni, water came out of the mouths of the gods. They looked at him every moment. Then with the welcome order of the king of the gods he took his seat. Accosted by the king of gods, saying "O Carrier of sacrificial offerings, how have you come by this highly distressful condition?" He sighing heavily replied.

"O King of gods, by thy command, which cannot be transgressed I went to Maheswara, engaged in sexual enjoyment with Gouri. Assuming the form of a pigeon and trembling greatly in fear, I approached the enemy of Smara. Knowing me under the false guise of a bird the omniscient Purusha, in great anger, thought of making a Homa with the fire burning on his fore-head. With great humility and pregnant words I eulogised him. He was pleased and propitiated with me. For who is not pleased when he is lauded?

Shankara, the Saviour of the refugees, saved me from the great fear of being devoured by the fire of anger. Then renouncing the embrace of the daughter of mountain in shame he desisted from the enjoyments of sexual intercourse. Immediately the mother of the universe, angered for the obstruction of her sexual pleasure, imprecated a curse on me. Being consumed by the energy thereof I could not bear the unbearable weight of the body. I am being consumed by that great and terrific energy. O Vasava, save my life and do me a good office."

Hearing those piteous words of Agni the king of gods was greatly sorry at heart and began to think of measures to avert the present evil. Then touching the body, of the Fire consumed by energy, with his fingers the lord of immortals said:—

"O Carrier of Havya, you yourself are a deity and the mouth of the Pitris and men. You please them with Swaha, Swadha & Vashatkar. Offering clarified butter to you the sacrificers, freed from sins, enjoy eternal heaven. O hutashana, offering Havi, sanctified with mantras to you, the ascetics attain Siddhi. Forsooth, you are the lord of asceticism. You carry many articles to the sun. They, converted into clouds, pour down rain which creates food stuff. Therefore you are protector of the world. You range the heart of the elements. They gain strength by you, they acquire longevity through you and therefore you give vitality to the world. For benefitting this celestial host you have been visited by this calamity. This danger is an object of pride to you since that wicked demon is injuring our cause. The goddess Bhagirathi has been pleased with our devotion. If you plunge your body into her water this your burning pain will be removed. O carrier of havya, be not depressed. Go to the Ganges. Speediness conduces to the success of necessary actions. That celestial stream is the watery form of Shambhu. She will transfer from you to herself the unbearable energy of Sambhu."

Saying it the king of gods stopped. Taking leave from him the Fire proceeded to the celestial stream. After going a little distance he reached the goddess Ganga, destroying the mass of sins. That celestial stream, like unto the stairs of heaven, is the presiding goddess of the celestial road. She destroys sins and saves the creatures from dangers. Virtue is stationed in the Ganges only, living in the matted locks of Mahesha, destructive of sins, and conferring emancipation to the race of Sagara. She has sprung from the lotus-foot of Vishnu and descended from the region of Brahma. With three streams she is continually purifying the three worlds.

Beholding Agni, from a distance, to approach, the ever delighted Surudhani with rising waves for her hands welcomed him for the accomplishment of his work. Swans swimming in her waters were emitting sweet notes. As if in those words she spoke to fire "I will remove your pain and do you good," With her heaving roars rising towards the bank the celestial Ganga went in advance to receive Agni. Thereupon stricken with burning pain Agni speedily plunged himself into the water of Bhagirathi. Do the persons, overpowered by dangers, delay in averting them? Plunging his body into the water of the exhaustion-removing, purifying, virtue-giving Ganga ever doing good, Agni was pacified. The Hutashana transferred to the water of Ganga the energy of Maheswara, the cause of his internal burning sensation. Bathed in that sacred water like unto nectarine streams the fire-god, highly pleased, departed for his own quarter. Bearing the unbearable seminal fluid of the destroyer of Smara, the etherial and sin-destroying Ganga began to suffer terribly. Assailed by thousands of scintillations of the fire of dissolution the acquatic animals, leaving that hot water, went elsewhere. By Rudra's energy the water of the Ganges became highly heated and swollen. With great difficulty she bore it. When the hot rays, the eyes of the world as it were, were about to rise in the month of Magha, the six Kirtikas came to the Ganges for bathing. Bathing in her thousands of white and sky-touching waves and performing their ablutions there the pious men attain heaven. She was as if declaring this. Strewn with Durva grass, Akshata and flowers, intended for the offerings of the adorations of well-bathed Munis, her banks assumed a great beauty. On her banks were seated yogis in Padma postures, engaged in the meditation of Brahma, fallen into yoga sleep and having serpents tied around their persons.

In some places of her banks, the Rishis, standing on thir toes and looking towards the solar disc, were engaged in the meditation of Brahma. Beholding the sacred streams of Ganga the six Kirtikas were highly pleased. What person is there to whose delight this river of nectarine streams does not conduce?

Thinking that a sight of her, whom the god of of gods carries on his crown is productive of virtue the six Kirtikas cherished a great reverence in their hearts. Bowing to her who gives emancipation and who flows from the foot of Vishnu, and shorn of sins they with delight and devotion chanted her glories. The six Kirtikas, with great devotion, began to serve Ganga who saves the three worlds, whom they have obtained by their good fortune, the very representative as it were of the emancipation of pious sages.

Having their sins washed off by her pure water, been well bathed, the six ascetic Kirtikas bathed there. Having bathed in that charming Mandakini on account of the fruition of their good luck they considered themselves highly pious and were greatly pleased.

As soon as they entered into the water of the Ganges, the seminal fluid of Mahadeva entered into their bodies. Bearing that unbearable and burning semem of Rudra they began to suffer greatly like unto persons sunk into an ocean of poison. Rising up from the Ganges they felt great exhaustion. And being unable to bear that semen they were as if being consumed by an internal fire. That semen of Siva entering into their womb from the river they soon conceived. When they perceived full well that they had concieved they were greatly sorry in fear of their husbands. On account of this incident they thought "Against our will this shameful and death-like misfortune has overtaken us." They all together began thus to bewail and lament. Thereupon, for fear of curse they threw that conception in a forest of reeds and went home. When they threw up in the sky that embryo, tender and lustrious like the rays of the moon, it, assuming an effulgence, defying hundreds of suns and setting at naugh the head of the moon-crested deity, was born with six faces.

---

## CANTO XI.

Thereupon on being bowed to and solicited by Indra and other celestials the celestial stream nursed that baby by giving it milk from her own breasts. Sucking every moment her breasts full of nectar that baby grew up like the digit of the moon. When the six Kirtikas began to serve him he acquired a form of indescribable beauty. The eyes of the Ganges, the Fire and the six Kirtikas were full of tears of joy. They began to quarrel amongst themselves to come by the celestial boy. In the meantime, ranging at will with Parvati, Shankara came there in a car swift like the mind. Beholding the boy of six faces, the daughter of the mountain and the lord of mountains cherished natural affection for him and their eyes were full of tears of joy. Thereupon the goddess Gouri said to the moon-crested Siva:—

"O lord, who is this celestial infant before us? Of what most fortunate man is he the son? What woman, the luckiest of her race, is his mother? This celestial Ganges, this fire and the six Kirtakas are shamelessly quarrelling amongst themselves, each of them saying "This is my son! This is my son." Whose, amongst them or amongst the Devas, Daityas, Gandharvas, Siddhas, Uragas and Rakshasas, son is this infant, the concentrated beauty of the universe? Tell me this, O lord."

Being thus accosted smilingly by his consort, dear like his life unto him out of curiosity, Maheshwara, knowing that an occasion for great felicity had arrived, gave vent to words conducive to pleasure.

"O mother of a heroe, this son, a great heroe and the delight of thee worlds, is yours. O auspicious lady, this son will do good unto the celestials. Who else but you can mother this most excellent, highly heroic, accomplished and most beautiful son? O worshipful lady, you are the source of auspiciousness to the world. It is really true. Consider well that ocean is the birth place of jems. Therefore listen attentively to his history. In great anger I discharged my irrepressible energy at Agni. By bathing in the Ganges he transferred it to her. Afterwards when the six Kirtikas went to bathe in the Ganges the seminal fluid passed into their body and they concieved. They threw the embryo in the forest of reed; from it is born this boy, as if the festivity of the entire universe, mobile and immobile.

O daughter of the mountain-chief, by this son, the most beautiful in the universe, you have been made the foremost of all good mothers. Do not delay; fill up your lap with this boy."

Hearing these words of Mahadeva, the creator of the three worlds, the plump-bodied Parvati, the protectress of the entire universe, in great delight got down from the car, saluted by the gods with hands on their crowns, stationed in the sky and became very anxious to recieve her son. Although Ganga, the six Kirtikas and fire bowed unto her with folded hands, still not noticing them, she affectionately took up the son on her lap, for people are maddened with joy on the birth of a son. Although the boy was sitting before her Parvati could not see him for her eyes were filled with tears of joy. But touching him with her fingers she experienced indescribable joy. With her body filled with surprise and joy and bathed in tears of joy she, on account of growing affection, cast her eyes on that beautiful boy, effulgent like the moon, who had come within her view. Seeing that boy for a short time she was, as if, desiring to have a thousand eyes for whose mind is not delighted after seeing a beautiful son? Holding those two tender hands which touch the backs of the submissive gods and demons Parvati took up that boy, beautiful like the rising full moon, on her lap.

Taking her son on her lap, the source of nectar, the lotus-faced goddess Parvati, adorable to the universe, became the foremost of all women having sons. When filled with affection and delight Parvati, the only mother of the universe, took him on her lap, milk began to ooze out from her breasts. Looked at by Surudhani and the six Kartikas, Shadanana, having six mothers, began to suck the breasts of Parvati, the mother of the entire universe. With her one mouth bathed in tears of joy Parvati, the consort of the moon-crested Siva, kissed his six faces, appearing like six lotuses on one stalk. As the golden mountain shines, holding the new moon in the east like unto fruit of a creeper, or a lotus of the heavenly stream, so Parvati with the boy on her lap appeared highly beautiful. The moon-crested Siva delightedly and carefully holding her hand, Parvati with her son on her lap, got upon the car touching the sky.

With his hairs stirring up in delight Maheshwara too, out of affection for his son, took him from the lap of the daughter of the mountain. Handing over that holy son, the only receptacle of joy, to her husband, the daughter of the mountain stood embracing her husband. Then in the quick-coursing car the moon-crested Siva returned home within a short time.

Thereupon stationed in his most beautiful mansion situate on the summit of the crystal mountain Mahadeva ordered all his ghosts to make festivities conducive to his own pleasure. The followers of Siva celebrated with great delight the birth of the son of the daughter of the mountain chief. The ghosts set up moveable golden gateways covered with Santanaka flowers in crystal palaces. On the occasion of that festival Gandharva and Vidyadhara women came to the palace of Parvati and ordered by her began to sing auspicious songs. With auspicious articles in their hands the Matris came there like mothers. And putting Durva grass and *akshata* on the head of the son of the daughter of the mountain they took him in their lap. Plunged into joy the Apsaras, when the trumpets were sounded, began to dance embracing the boy, in accompaniment with the music of Vina, displaying various gestures. Delightful wind blew on the occasion of that festival, the waters were clean and the quarters put on a delightful appearance. Bugles were then sounded in heaven accompanied with the blowing of conchs. And the cars of celestials pouring torrents of flowers, moved about in the sky. Thus the festival on the birth of the son of Maheswara and the daughter of the mountain was celebrated over the entire universe; only the goddess of Taraka's prosperity trembled.

With various childish sports conducive to their pleasure the Kumara stole the minds of the mountain-god and mountain-daughter. To whose pleasure the play of a child does not conduce? With a single mouth Maheshwara and Parvati respectively kissed the six faces of this son in which teeth were not grown. Sometimes slipping and again walking firm, sometimes trembling and again walking straight the boy increased the joy of his parents. Covered with dust while playing in the court-yard, smiling without any cause and uttering incoherent words the boy used to go to the lap of his parents and increase their joy. The boy used sometimes to hold the horns of Siva's carrier, the clotted hairs of his father and sharp horns of Shringi and thus conduce to the pleasure of Hara and Parvati. On a certain occasion going to the lap of his father the infant son of Mahesha used to count the teeth of the serpents around his neck, saying, one, nine, two, ten, five and seven. Sometimes, the boy putting his finger into the mouth of the skulls engarlanding Siva and catch the teeth resembling pearl-drops. Again he used to plunge his limbs into the water of the stream flowing on Siva's head; and when his hands were cold he used to warm them in the fire kept on the fore-head of his sire. Again putting obliquely on his neck the moon hanging on the crown of Shambhu wearing matted locks he used to kiss it. Thus did Hara and Parvati spend day and night with great delight witnessing the childish sports of their son. Increasing the deep joy of his parents with various lovely childish sports the boy attained youth within six days and learnt from Mahadeva all the scriptures and the use of all weapons.

## CANTO XII.

Thereupon oppressed by the wily Asuras, and accordingly stricken with great anxiety Sachi's lord, along with all the celestials, approached the enemy of Andhaka as a thirsty chataka begs water from a cloud. In fear of the haughty Asuras the king of gods could not range all over the etherial way. Still imperceptibly and with great adieu he ascended from the cloud on the mount Kailasha painted with the foot-steps of Hara and Gouri. Leaning on Matali's hand Indra got down from his cloudy car and proceeded towards the abode of the trident-handed deity like unto a thirsty person approaching a stream in summer. Although going alone still he saw a multiplicity of his own forms being reflected on the crystal aud thus reached the house of the Lord. The king of gods arrived at the gate of Shankara, constructed artistically with various jems. Highly terrific Nandi was standing there with a golden rod in hand. Seeing the king of gods all on a sudden Nandi, with a golden rod hanging from his waist, welcomed him and conducted him to the court of Maheshwara.

Thereupon commanded by the Lord with the contraction of his eye-brows Nandi preceded the gods and their king and conducted them to the abode of the three-eyed deity. Thereupon the thousand-eyed deity saw Mahadeva in that assembly-hall adorned with various jems and occupied by

Chanda, Bhringi and other leading goblins having diverse forms. Lighted with jems of serpents hanging on his head and wearing matted locks he shone there like the highly elevated peak of the mount Sumeru filled with burning metals. A garland of skulls was shining on his neck. Parvati was seated on his lap. And situate on his matted locks the goddess Ganga was as if smiling with her white foams. He held on his head the moon which shed lustre on the Ganga bearing its reflection, the serpents and the quarters with its snow-white and trembling rays.

Overpowering the sun and his other two moon-like eyes, the fire like unto that of the universal dissolution which reduced Madana into ashes was shining in the eye that was on his forehead. With the great lustre of his blue throat, as if a necklace of blue jems has been sportively put there by Gouri Shankara was shining there. Stationed on his two ears and lighting up all around with rays set with valuable jems, the sun and the moon were as if serving him in the shape of two ear-rings. His limbs, covered with a thick skin, like that of a huge elephant, covered with ashes of gods and Asuras at the time of universal dissolution were appearing there like the mount Himalaya. He had as if in his hand the skull vessel of Brahma, on his limbs the garland of Vishnu's bones and that of the bones of the celestials on his neck and held the trident destructive of wars. He wore a garland of skulls, revived with hope, round his neck. And reviving by the nectarine currents coming down from his head those skulls were reciting the Vedas. The daughter of the mountain chief, of the hue of molten gold, was seated on his lap and for which he looked like an autumnal cloud accompanied with lightning. He held by two fingers the unbearable trident Pinaka which consumed the Asura Pura who made the wives of the demon Gaya widowed. He was seated on a excellent seat with a golden foot stool set with various precious jems. Two Ganas where fanning him on two sides with chowries. Other Ganas, devotedly learning the use of weapons, were looking at him. Amvika, with the corner of her cloth, was fanning the Kumara. And casting his looks on him Mahadeva was experiencing great delight.

Beholding thus the lord of the daughter of the mountain there the lord of Sachi stood stupified for some time, for whose mind is not agitated on seeing the repositary of effulgence? With his thousand beautiful eyes resembling full blown lotuses the king of gods began to look at Mahadeva for some time. Thereat it appeared that there stood a tree covered with blossoming flowers. Seeing Shankara with his thousand eyes the king of gods regarded himself fortunate and thought within himself :—These my thousand eyes used only to look at my dear Sachi formerly. Now looking at Mahadeva they have justified their existence. Therefore beholding Kumara armed with powerful weapons, seated by Mahadeva like a mount of gold Purandera began to hope for victory. Placing the golden rod on his breast and folding his hands Nandi said :—"O thou having a blue throat! O thou having three eyes, O Maheshwara! the thousand-eyed king of celestials is standing before thee seeking an opportunity for bowing unto thee. Be thou propitiated with him. The object of thy grace stands before thee, do thou extend thy grace unto him."

Thereupon with love and delight the destroyer of Tripura favoured Indra, the destroyer of Asuras and adored of the celestials, with his nectarine looks. Then taking down in humble devotion his head with Parijata flowers dropping from his crown, the foremost of gods, the deity of thousand eyes, the only adorable one in heaven, bowed unto Mahadeva, the only god of the universe. Having bowed respectfully unto Mahadeva, worthy of the adoration of all the worlds, the king of heaven and gods was crowned with consummate success. Thereupon lowering down their respective heads with delighted eyes the other celestials, endued with reverential faith, one by one appeared before his foot-stool and bowed unto the enemy of Smara. Afterwards on a golden seat being brought before by the Ganas at the command of their Lord the king of celestials sat on it and experienced great delight. Who is not pleased in receiving a recognition from his master? Thereupon with a slight smile Maheshwara looked at other celestials and honored them. Then seated all together within his view they attained to great delight.

Seeing the pale countenance with pity of Indra and other gods seated with folded hands before him, who were being oppressed by the Asuras and whose wives had been ravished by them Mahadeva said :— "O heroes! O deities dwelling in heaven! great is the power of your arms. Why then are your countenances pale like a lotus stricken with frost? Despite great piety the dwellers of heaven have been divorced from their regions. Have you all relinguished your respective superiority? Casting off their honor, wealth and celestial homes why the great gods are ranging on earth like ordinary mortals? Like unto virtue declining with the increase of sin why Yama and other gods have left their beautiful celestial homes which other creatures cannot acquire? O celestials! why do you look pale like distressed persons in the presence of the destroyer of Pura. The Demon Taraka has conquered the three worlds. Have you been greatly assailed by him? Relate every thing clearly to me. I alone am able to avert the defeat inflicted by that great Asura. What else save clouds can quench the forest-fire?

Hearing those words of the great god Mahadeva, the destroyer of Manmatha, the deities headed by

Indra were greatly relieved and delighted. Signs of joy appeared on their smiling countenances. Thereupon after the termination of Siva's speech the king of the celestials began his own in that advantageous moment. For if words are said in a proper time they yeild fruits.

"O lord, thou art the effulgent lamp of knowledge destructive of the quality of darkness. Present, past and future and all that is is within the ken of thy knowledge. O lord, dost thou not know that we have been dislodged from our respective stations by the terrible and the highly powerful Asura Taraka always oppressing the immortals? Having obtained an infalliable boon from the Creator the terrific and the highly powerful demon Taraka is regarding Indra, the enemy of Jambhu and other gods as straw. When I lauded the Grand father with verses he said that the son of the enemy of Smara would go out to the field as general and destroy the Asuras. Now the gods, residing in heaven, are suffering great pain, like that caused by a mace cutting to the quick, caused by the commands and oppressions of that irrepressible demon. Here is present before us the heroe who will remove the misery of the gods after destroying in battle that great Asura like unto a mace stuck to the heart of the Prosperity of three worlds. O lord, let the quarters resound with the cries of the wives of the great Asura, on his head being cut off by the sharpened arrows of thy son discharged in battle. Having that great Asura as food to the beasts of prey in the battle-field may thy son loosen the tresses of celestial damsels kept captives in heaven."

Hearing the words of the king of celestials and filled with anger caused by the atrocities of that demon the destroyer of Smara, showing favour unto the gods, again said :—

"Hear my words, O king of gods and deities. Well armed for the work of gods Kumara will in no time try to do you good. Although I was controlling my passion still I espoused the hand of the daughter of the mountain. The only cause of it is that a heroic son, begotten by me, will kill that Asura in the battle-field. Therefore appoint him as your genernal for killing your enemy. May the king of gods along with deties again sanctify the celestial region." Then the divine lord of Bhavani blessed his son who was anxious for a battle saying "Achieve victory in the war of gods." It is a great virtue to persons devoted to their father. The lord of gods and brutes having said thus about the war, the daughter of the mountain was greatly pleased on hearing of the prowess of her son. Women, giving birth to heroes, enjoy great pleasure on witnessing the prowess of their sons in battle. Having obtained Kartikeya, the powerful son of Uma's lord, the destroyer of the collyrium in the eyes of the enemy's wives, and the saviour of the world, the king of gods was highly pleased. Who is not elated with joy when his desire is crowned with success ?

---

## CANTO XIII.

Thereupon having put on a dress for journey and about to be followed by the celestials Kumar touched with his hand the feet of Mahadeva the preserver of the three worlds. Maheshwara welcomed him by blessing. "O heroe ! O child ! reinstate in battle the gods in their respective positio ns." Then bowing humbly his head he saluted the feet of his mother. With the tears of joy of his mother the auspicious sprinkling ceremony of the great heroe was performed. Embracing her son warmly and smelling his head the daughter of the mountain, ever fond of her son, said " Defeating the enemies make good my name "*the mother of heroes.*" Having saluted Siva and Uma with a reverent heart the General Kumar Kartikeya, the source of misery to proud Danavas, set out for the celestial region. Then having bowed unto Uma and Mahadeva and circumambulated them the leading celestials followed Kumara. The deities endued with burning effulgence going in anger, the sky, even in day time, appeared to have been covered with luminous stars. The beautiful Kumar proceeded in their midst like the moon amongst stars and other luminous bodies. Passing over the starry way in a moment Indra and other deities arrived with Kumara at the region of the seven Rishis. Being unable to enter immediately into heaven, seen after a long time, for fear of the great Asura, the gods tarried outside for some time. They quarrelled amongst themselves about their entering into heaven occupied by their enemy, saying "You go first. I wfll not go before." Kumar was sportively marking the haste of the gods and his eyes were expanded with joy. The celestials, stricken with the fear of the enemy, fixed their eyes on him. With his moon-like countenance lighted up with the rays of smile that heroe, preceding them all and awaiting the arrival of Taraka, addressed the celestials saying.

"O ye immortals! do not fear. Enter fearlessly into heaven. Let that great Asura, the enemy of the celestials, seen by Death himself, appear in my view. Let my arrows immediately make a feast of his blood, whose two arms have been elated with pride for drawing the hairs of the goddess of prosperity of heaven. May this my unmitigated power cut off the head of the enemy and conduce to your happiness."

These words of the son of the enemy of Andhaka whose mind was bent upon killing the enemy greatly gladdened the king of the celestials. And after a long time their lotus-like countenances were expanded with joy. Then greatly delighted the thousand-eyed deity rubbed him with his raiment.

Filled with great joy, Brahma, assailed by the Asuras, kissed his six faces with his four mouths having eyes filled with tears of joy. Narada and other celestial Saints approved highly of his speeah bearing a most excellent signification. In order to encourage that hero of great energy the Devas, with Gandharvas, Vidyadharas and Siddhas, cast off their fear and pleased him with saying "O heroe, be thou crowned with success." Then eulogising the son of the killer of Tripura with exclamations of "Well said," they with their golden raiments touched his person. Thereupon the gods followed the son of the daughter of the mountain who was desirous of defeating Purandara's enemy as the ghosts follow the enemy of Smara. Thereupon they reached the celestial river the water of which was rendered twany by the washing of the dyes of the celestial damsels. Some going before began to describe with pleasure the watery sports of boars wounded by the trunks of the elephants of quarters.

Preceding Kartikeya saw the ethereal river of heaven watering again and again the canals dug around the trees grown on its bank. Her banks were covered with altars having pillows set with jems by the celestial damsels sportively ranging in the sky and sweet-speeched like golden geese. Covered with black bees drawn by the perfume of her water, and filaments of golden lotuses loosened by the movements of golden geese her water appeared red.

On her waves were reflected the forms of the celestials collected on her bank out of curiosity. And seeing them the passers-by experienced great delight.

Beholding that celestial stream after a long time as if not seen before the king of gods had his eyes expanded with surprise. Approaching that Mandakini adored of the celestials, Kumara, placing his folded hands on his crown, lauded and saluted her. Shaking the full blown lotuses and embracing the waves the wind served the Kumara after removing the drops of perspiration from his forehead. While passing on Kartikaya, the son of the enemy of Smara, saw before him Indra's pleasure-garden Nandana, containing various trees the branches of which were broken. When Kartikeya saw that garden the beauty of which was despoiled by the wicked Danavas his face put on a grim visage and his eyes became reddened.

Thereupon Kumara beheld Amaravati, the essence of the entire universe. At that time the celestial cars were not moving about there—all the pleasures thereof were spoiled and that city, the cream of the entire universe, was in a pitiable condition. The prosperity of the city was pilfered.. by the enemies and she looked poorly on every side. Seeing her like a helpless woman Kumara was stricken with pity. Seeing in that city the atrocities of the enemy of gods he was filled with anger, and mortification. Anxious or battle and looking at Amaravati in that wretched plight he entered there along with the celestials. Seeing the crystal palaces, standing on the expanded fangs of huge serpents, the pillars of which were broken down by the teeth of the kings of demons he was filled with great mortification. The golden lotuses, engraved in that city, were spoiled with the temporal juice of the elephants of quarters——the sappire altars were filled with golden geese and the lakes were covered with reeds. Witnessing these oppressions of the enemies Kumara was worked up with sorrow and shame. Preceding the king of gods took him to his own palace Vaijayanta, the pillars of which were broken by the tusks of the elephants, and jems were covered with cobwebs. The king of gods himself showing the way Kumara, followed by other gods, entered there by stairs set with jems. Thereupon having benedictory ceremonies performed by the Munis, Kumara entered inside the palace decorated with garlands of Parijata flowers and gate-ways beautified with natural desire-fullfilling trees.

Having circumambulated the great saint Kashyapa, the originator of gods and demons, Kartikeya saluted him by bending low his six heads. Afterwards he touched with his head the feet of the wife of that great Rishi, Aditi, adorable unto the world. Thereupon Kashyapa and Aditi, the mother of Suras, blessed him who was desirous of defeating Taraka saying "Defeat the Asura Taraka in battle."

Then Kumar saluted the deities, living under the protection of Aditi, who had come there to see him. The gods welcomed him with blessings. Then Kumara saluted Indra's queen Sachi, the daughter of Puloma. She too received him with blessings. Then approaching the seven Mothers, Aditi and others Kumara saluted them with reverence. They als• blessed him. Here Indra and other gods assembled and filled with joy appointed him as their Generalissimo. While having accepted the command of the celestial army Kumara, the son of Hara •f endless enegies, inspired the gods with the hope of victory over their enemy, they finding an apportunity for battle cast off all sorrow.

---

## CANTO XIV.

Thereupon Kartikeya, the son of the enemy of Andhaka, ever anxious to enter into battle and desirous of victory, began to make preparations for war along with the celestials for destroying the great Asura Taraka in battle by force. Then the great bowman Kartikeya ascended a huge car by name *Vijitwar*, swift like the mind, and irrepressible like victory hard to acquire. Some one held at that time over his head the beautiful and well-built golden umbrella which saved the prosperity of heaven from dangers and assailed that of the Asuras. Some fanned him with chowries beautiful like the rays of the autumnal moon. And preceding Kinnaras, and Charanas chanted aloud the glories of Kartikeya anxious to fight. Putting on a war-dress, holding his infalliable thunder-bolt which had cut off the wings of the mountains, and riding his elephant Airavata like unto a huge crystal mountain the king of heaven followed him. Riding his infuriated lamb, huge like a mountain summit, blazing the more in anger begotten by hatered and inspired with greater energy the fire-god followed him. Holding a dreadful rod and riding an infureated bull, huge-bodied like a black mountain and capable of piercing rocks with its horns Yama, desirous of fighting, followed the celestial General. Riding a goblin Nairita, worked up with terrific anger on account of hatered and elated with pride, followed for battle the son of Andhaka' enemy. Riding a Makara huge like a gate and dreadful, Varuna, endued with youthful zeal and holding his noose followed Kumara, mad after fighting. Riding his deer which can pass over Kailasha and other mounts in a moment and going like wind, the fierce and great warrior Kuvera followed Kumara. Holding a huge mace which was desirous of drinking the blood of the enemies, and riding a conveyance carried by men he followed the Lord's son who was about to plunge himself into the ocean of war. Riding huge bulls white like snow-clad mountains the Pinakis, who bind their clotted locks with huge serpents and hold blazing tridents in the battle-field, followed Kumara. Other dwellers of heaven too, out of reverence for the battle, riding their most excellent carriers and having countenances beaming with joy, followed Kumara.

Thereupon Kartikeya, son of Trident-handed Siva, led the great celestial army to the battle-field. It consisted of lofty golden standards, moving umbrellas of variegated colours, clatter of car-wheels and the sound of bells around the necks of elephants. The lustre of this army lighted up the quarters. The quarters, sky and earth were filled with their war-cries, and thick-set flags. The quarters and the sky were filled with the sound of drums at which the prosperity of the Asuras trembled. Resounding with the sound of drums like unto the roaring of the ocean and capable of causing abortion of Asura women, the sky, assailed with the dust raised by the soldiers, was as if making a dreadful noise. Dust of golden mountains was raised by horse hoops, spread by cars and the ears of the elephants, caught by clouds and dispersed by the wind. And gradually the sky was filled with it. Dust of gold was raised in the valley by the hoops of horses and scattered over all the quarters by the gusts of wind made it impossible to discern the directions. Being all over the army, beneath, upwards, before, in the rear and on all sides the dust of gold defeated the rays of the newly-risen sun. Dust of gold raised by the soldiers shone brilliantly in the sky. It appeared thereat that twany clouds had risen in the red dye of the untimely evening. Seeing their own reflections on the golden ground and mistaking them for others rising from the nether region the elephants began to strike them fiercely with their tusks. Rendered tawny with golden dusts and going slowly the celestial elephants going to the mount of pure gold saw their own reflections before. Shaking the forest skirts with their noise the army, of the king of immortals anxious to fight a great battle, descended from the golden mountain. The loud cries of the war-elephants increased by the trinkling of their bells could not arouse the lions sleeping at ease in the caves of the mount. Are the lions called kings of beasts because they are not terrified by the sound of bugles and its echo in the caves as well as by the sound of huge cars? The war-cries of the soldiers rending even the mountains maddened the lions. In fear of being struck by the celestial host the deer fled away but the lions came out of the caves and stood fearlessly at their mouth. Filled with curiosity people delightedly looked at Amaravati. The army did not extend all over the vast and extensive foot of the mount of celestials. The huge army marched covering the earth. It was not measured anywhere and proceeded towards heaven. It appeared like the extensive and moving city of Gandharvas. When he roar of the army entered into ears it appeared that a great sound extending all over the world had arisen on account of the churning of the ocean of milk. The ears were covered with noise of elephants, neighings of horses and the rattle of car-wheels. The dust raised by the soldiers stuck for some time to the hairs, eyes, eye-lashes and breasts of women kept in prison by the Asuras, and to their flags, horses, cars and elephants. The dust of the army covered the sky and the sun. When the dust assumed the form of new clouds the golden standards rising up to sky, looked like lightning. The vast interstice between the heaven and earth being covered with dust people began to think that it was coming either from up or down. But no body could ascertain the cause. On account of the spreading of the dust, so thick that even a needle's point could not pierce it, the vision of creatures could not extend on any side. On account of the roars of the elephants of quarters being resounded on cars and of the neighing of horses it appeared that the sky was roaring. Not even finding time to breathe on account of the roars of infuriated elephants, neighs of tall horses, and the rattle of the wheels of moving cars decorated with standards the sky was as if greatly assailed. The quarters as if became talkative by the terrific roars of elephants, tinkling of bells and cries of heroes. A river was immediately created by the temporal juice trickling from the infuriated elephants. It was converted into mud by the dust raised by the hoofs of the horses; and when the cars passed over it it became solid earth. The movements of the horses lowered some places and elevated others. But the cars and elephants levelled them all. The sound of bugles capable of rending the huge mountains which was resounded in the sky and the extremities of the quarters terrified the world as if with the roaring of the ocean. The flags obstructing the sky and quarters on being shaken by the wind, and the golden bells making a tinkling sound were plunged into the ocean of dust. The incessant ringing of the bells and the roars of the infuriated elephants were clouded by the sound of drums. When the clothes of the women of the quarters in menses dropped down by the terrific cries of the soldiers all the quarters were clouded with dust and the sun disappeared. Attacking by force the women of quarters and soiling them with dust the soldiers set up a terrible roar by the echo of the sound of bugles. When the elephants like unto moving mountains, covered the sky it appeared that thick clouds were bent down on earth by the weight of water of the illimitable oceans, roaring terribly at the time of the universal dissolution and poured their contents on mountains filling up the space between the sky and earth.

## CANTO XV.

THE rumour that Indra, the destroyer of Bala, is coming out with Kartikeya, the son of Andhaka's enemy, at the head of his army, shook the heart of the Asuras. Hearing that the son of Manmatha's enemy shining in victoroy, was coming out with victorious army of gods the minds of the leading Asuras were greatly agitated. Placing their hands on their crests the guards said to the king of Daityas :—

"O king of Asuras, himself desirous of battle, Jambha's enemy Indra is coming with the son of Smara's enemy."

The king of Asuras began to laugh tauntingly saying "I have made slaves of the three worlds. Sachi's lord has defeated me many times and he will vanquish me this time with the help of Girisha's son."

With his lips trembling that proud and fiercely powerful Asura, Taraka, ordered his Generals to get ready for battle, with a view to conquer the three worlds. Armed for battle the Generals began to wait outside the gate of the courtyard filled with submissive kings. Many commanders, elated with the pride of churning the ocean, were waiting there on horse-back. When pointed out by the warder they saluted the king of Daityas at which he was highly pleased. Thereupon the Asura Taraka proceeded towards the battle-field in his terrible and huge car, the rattle of whose wheels caused the temporal juice of the elephants of quarters to ooze, which could destroy the strength of Indra and was capable of being obstructed by the great ocean and mountain only. Then a huge army followed the king of Daityas. It set up a roar terrible like that of the ocean agitated at the time of universal dissolution. Its flags obstructed the rays of the sun. And the dust raised by it covered the sun and the extremeties of the quarters. The dust raised by the soldiers of the Asura king while proceeding towards the celestials, increased the whiteness of the teeth of the elephants of quarters and created mud in jars full of sacred water.

The mountain caves of the great Asura and the sky were agitated with sound of drums. Rising at the roars of the huge army of the enemy of gods the celestial river washed the houses of heaven with numberless waves. The evil omens, as if the standards of Death himself, appeared before the Asuras who were about to march for the battle-field. Flying above the army of the Asura-chief, dreadful-looking celestial birds began to obstruct the rays of the sun. It presaged the sure destruction of the Daityas. Then the wind, blowing high, broke into pieces the umbrella rods and disturbed great men, horses, elephants, and huge cars. Then went before them huge serpents, dark like collyrium and of dreadful forms, vomitting poisonous fire and presaging evil. United with the huge serpents the sun began to shed fierce rays, as if out of his enmity towards his enemy, the great Asura, he was going with his mouth wide open. Assembled together and looking towards the solar disc the jackals began to cry hideously being desirous of drinking blood, after the termination of the war of the king of celestials. Dropped down during the day stars began to fall around the army of Asuras. Thereat people thought that a great disaster, destructive of the lives of Asuras, was present. Rising up with their rays, lighting up the sky up to the extremities of the quarters, and rending them with fierce sound fere-brands began to drop down from the cloudless sky. The sky began to pour down burning embers, blood and bones. And displaying smoky flames it showed brownish dust in the quarters. Terrible gusts of winds, setting up sounds like unto those at the time of universal dissolution and capable of piercing the ear-holes, and striking down the summits of mountains filled up with the dust the earth, sky and interstices between the quarters. There took place such a terrible earth-quake rending the mountains and agitating the oceans so that huge elephants shook before the army of the enemies of the celestial, horses dropped down and people fell embracing one another. Collected together and looking up to the solar disc the dogs began to yell hideously before the Asuras.

Even beholding these evil omens presaging a terrible result, the wily king of Asuras Taraka, influenced by an evil destiny, did not, in anger, desist from setting out for the battle. Although he was prevented by many Asuras on seeing these evil omens still he went on. For useless is the advice of the good unto him blindly following evil ways. The umbrella of the great Asura was struck down on the ground. It so appeared then that the drinking bowl of death, made of silver, was placed on the ground. His crown was torn knowing as if that the severing of his head was certain. And by the continuous dropping of pearls it was, as it were, weeping pouring drops of tears. Anticipating the certain death of the Asura-chief although prevented by his followers on all sides the vultures came near his head as if being desirous of taking it. People saw a huge serpent, dark as collyrium, spreading lustre of the jem on his hood, hiss as if desirous of vomitting venom. Dreadful fire, originating from the axles of his car, consumed the hair cowries and quivers. Although repeatedly visited by these evil omens, still the king of Asuras, worked up with pride, did not desist from setting out for war. Then an etherial voice of the Maruts was heard.

"O Asura, maddened with pride, do not vaunt of the strength of thy arms in a combat with the son of Shankara and ever victorious Indra. As nocturnal darkness cannot overpower the sun so the great Asuras will not be able to defeat Kartikeya born six days before. So thy quarrel with him will do thee injury. Dost thou expect victory over him in battle who has made holes in the great mountain Kroucha which stands clouding the sky with hundreds of summits and obstructing the way of the guardians of the quarters. In sooth it is an imppossibility. It is impossible for thee to fight with that lion-like heroe, the glory of the three worlds, with whom even Jamadagnya does not wish to fight,—Jamadagnya the night of death unto the Kshatryas, who having learnt the science of war from Siva sprinkled himself with the blood of the thighs of kings for twenty one times."

Hearing this most important ethereal speech that great Asura was beside himself with anger and possessed by pride did not hear. Shaking the three worlds with the weight of his army he proceeded towards heaven. Then the sky-ranging deities said:—

"O proud Asura, do not show your pride before the great prowess of Mahadeva's son. Seeking refuge with this only heroe of the universe live at ease for a tong time."

Thereupon the king of Daityas replied:—"O ye deities ranging in the sky, what do you say, taking the opposite side of the Asuras. Alas, immediately forgetting the pain inflicted by my arrows you will take to your heels. Stationed in the sky and depending upon the strength of a boy, six days old, what are you speaking harshly like wicked dogs in the night of a Kartika month? This infant son of the ascetic will surely meet with destruction. As even an innocent man is killed by keeping company with a thief, so after destroying you all first I will afterwards kill that innocent boy."

The king of Asuras after having said this the sky-ranging gods, holding huge daggers, fled away in fear, each striking the other with his knee-joints.

Thereupon laughing hideously in pride and placing his shining sword in the sheath the king of Asuras said to his charioteer "Do you soon drive the car where the king of gods is."

Thus commanded he drove the car swift as the mind and the Asura Taraka reached the fore-part of the dreadful celestial army. Beholding that vast celestial army and being anxious to play with his huge arms the king of Asuras was filled with great delight. Worked up with a desire to fight the followers of the Daitya went on as swiftly as the mind. Do the heroes ever make delay in battle?

Plunging themselves into the ocean of soldiers, throwing up their arms the soldiers of the Asura began to recite their own names. Beholding before the army of the Asura like a vast ocean all the gods were worked up with anxiety. But the result of the future battle was perceptible in the corner of the eye of the son of Smara's enemy the commander-in-chief of the celestial army. Seeing the celestial solders stricken with anxiety on beholding the enemy's army the General Kartikeya looked with graceful eyes at them inorder to ascertain his own strength. Seeing that great heroe in battle Indra and other gods exclaimed "I will defeat the enemy in battle," and began to display great zeal. Who is there who does not display his power on being united with the foremost of heroes. The car-warriors respectfully reciting their names the soldiers of the holder of thunder-bolt as well as those of his enemy took up their arms.

There arose a great tumult from the two armies of the gods and demons, extending far and wide and worked up with anger like unto that of the two oceans heaving and going beyond their banks at the time of dissolution. If appeared that inorder to make profuse presents unto death a great tumult, capable of rending the mountains, filled the belly of the universe.

---

## CANTO XVI.

Thereupon displaying their respective arms the celestial and Asura hosts began to fight a terrible battle. The foot soldiers confronted the foot, the car-warriors fought with the car-warriors, the infantry with the infantry, the elephant-warriors with other elephant-warriors. The panegyrists began to sing the history of the heroes. Worked up with eulogy the the heroes, without spending a moment, began to fight. When the heroes began to fight with one another their bodies increased with the joy of war and thereat their coats of mail dropped down from their persons. With coats of mail sundered mercilessly the sky and the quarters were rendered brown as if with cotton. Covered with blood, the swords of the heroes effulgent like the rays of the sun, appeared like so many lightnings. Arrows shot by clever warriors, emitting flames from their mouths like dreadful serpents covered the sky. Piercing deeply the body the arrows of the bowmen, without blood in their mouths, dropped down at a distance on the ground. The arrows first struck down the elephants piercing their body and then dropped down amongst the hostile warriors: the sky being strewn with thick and blazing arrows the car-warriors amongst the gods went elsewhere. Struck with the arrows of the warriors and being bewildered the sky began to make a hoarse sound in the shape of the war-cries of the Generals. Tempted to drink the blood of the warriors, engaged in the action, the arrows, shot off bows drawn to ears, dropped down at a distance. The heroes holding the unsheathed swords in their hands, they, appearing as the so many mouths of the battle by their lustre, began to laugh. The swords, bathed in blood, dancing in the palms of the warriors it appeared that lightnings manifested themselves in the vast battle-field clouded with dust. The burning effulgence of the persons of the leading car-warriors moved in the sky of battle like the rays of the sun. At the terrible war-cries of the assembled warriors some dropped down from the horses and others became insensible. Encountering their hostile combatants some heroes taking pleasure in battle were filled with joy. The cowards fled from the battle-field in dismay. Moving about and fighting with other heroes and calling them by names some warriors said " I have settled to fight you first." Some warriors struck at the arms of others coming towards them from all sides with hairs standing on end. The pearls dropped from the trappings of elephants and looked like seeds sown in the battle-field.

Terrified at the war-cries of the heroes, the elephants, not even controlled by the strokes of the hook began to fly away to the end of the quarter. Running in the battle-field, the huge-elephants, with bodies wounded with shafts, scattered the warriors and threw them into the ocean of blood. Confronting the enemies, some warriors, standing on huge cars in the rivers of blood, began to discharge arrows. The horses, having their heads severed with swords, dropped down not before having struck down the enemies whose heads were cut off with daggers. Falling down the heads of heroes, cut off by arrows, ran towards the enemies biting their lips with teeth. Holding the heads, of the leading warriors cut off with crescent-shaped arrows with their teeth the hawks began to fly away, covering all the quarters. Although the elephant-riders were wounded with arrows still the elephants began to move about; and it appeared thereat that the mountains were being shaken by the wind of dissolution. When the elephant-riders, in anger came between the infantry and cavalry the latter began to slaughter the former with Prashas. The fire, originating from the clashing of the tusks of the elephants began to consume all on a sudden the elephant-warriors killed by the weapons of the enemies. When the elephants, in anger, threw up the foot-soldiers with their trunks, their master, seated on them killed the enemies, thus thrown up, by cutting them in twain with their swords. The elephants caught the warriors and threw them at a distance. As soon as they were dead their souls held the celestial damsels by the neck. Weapons stole away the trunks which the infantry had cut off with their sharp swords. When the foot-soldiers were thrown up towards heaven by the elephants with their trunks crimson-hued celestial damsels came and covered the welkin. When the elephants thus began to fight the combatants killed one another with their weapons. Seeing the elephant riders swoon away the bowmen and horse-soldiers began to wait for sometime in expectation of an engagement. Desirous of cutting off the trunks of the wicked elephants with their swords the infantry began to get upon them piercing their tusks. Cutting the four legs of the elephants although the foot soldiers went under them they quickly came out before they dropped down.

Although caught by infuriated elephants the heroes killed them with their swords and remained themselves unhurt. One horse-soldier striking another such with his weapon, could not know before he was wounded that he was cut on his breast by the Prasa of the falling combatant. The huge horse, with his eyes dilated in fear, did not leave the body of the warrior covered with wounds even after he had dropped down dead. By the huge Pasa which he had formerly in his hand, the heroe, seated firm on horse back, although killed by his enemy, seemed alive and moving about in the battle-field with Prasa in his hand. Although severed with a sharp sword, the horse-soldier, before he swooned away, tried to kill his combatant in anger. When striking each other in anger both the heroes dropped down on earth they began to fight with knives or closed one another with arms or by holding one another's hairs. Setting formerly arrows to their bows, car-warriors, firmly seated, appeared alive although killed by other car-warriors. One car-warrior, seeing another fallen in swoon, desisted from striking him but waited in expectation of an engagement till he regained conscious ness. Two car-warriors, holding most excellent weapons, killed by each other, went to heaven and began to fight again for one Apsara. When the heads of the two heroes were chopped off with crescent-shaped arrows the sky-rangers saw their bodies dancing on earth. When trumpets were struck in the battle-field rendered slippery with blood goblin women and trunkless demons began to dance with great difficulty. Thus when the encounter between the gods and demons began a stream of blood flowed in the battle-field in which the elephants were like banks. With his eyes reddened in anger and frowning the king of Asuras came before the guardians of the quarters with a desire to fight with them.

## CANTO XVII.

When worked with a desire to sport in the battle-field Kartikeya, the commander-in-chief of the celestial army came before the guardians of the quarters, maddened with the fury of battle, assembled in the sky and quarters darkened with arrows. Then laughing hideously, the Asura-chief Taraka covered all the quarters with a down pour of arrows by which it appeared that clouds covered a huge mountain with incessant showers. As Garudas tear into pieces the serpents so the sharp arrows discharged by Indra and other guardian deities of quarters in the battle-field sundered into atoms the shafts of the king of Asuras. Like unto fire covering the quarters and sky the king of Asuras too, with burning arrows, with his name written thereon with grass, cut off the shafts of the celestial soldiers. The arrows, which were discharged by the Asura chief moving about and burning in anger in the battle-field, assuming terrific forms like raging serpents, fettered the leading celestials. Bound by the Asura in serpentine nooses and sighing heavily they desisted from fighting. In order to avert the evil the guardians of the quarters approached Kartikeya. Released from the calamity of being fettered by serpentine nooses by favourable looks of the son of Tripura's enemy they began to serve Kumara desirous of achieving a great victory.

Thereupon burning like the fire of anger the large-armed celestial enemy Taraka said to his charioteer :—"The gods headed by Indra bound by me with serpentine nooses have been released by the looks of the infant son of Mahesha. Leaving them I will offer sacrifice of beasts to the battle-field. Therefore drive my car to the Shambhu's son. I will see how much strength that proud Kurmar holds on his arms."

The charioteer drove his car making a rattle deep like the muttering of clouds. It proceeded slowly on the mud caused by flesh, bones and blood. Seeing that car of the celestial enemy come with a terrific form at the time of grinding the enemies like a huge mountain shaken by the wind at the time of universal dissolution the celestial soldiers began to tremble in fear. Seeing the soldiers of the deities of the quarters thus terrified approach Kartikeya anxious to sport in battle the terrific lord of Daityas Taraka, who held a bow with great prowess, said :—

"O weaver son of Sambhu, desist soon from this work which causes uneasiness unto the king of celestials. Am I afraid of the attack of your arms tender like new lotuses and unused to victories? You are the only and best son of Girisha and Gouri. Why will you die a premature death in the net of my arrows? Therefore no use of a battle. Flying from the battle-field in my fear fill up the tender laps of thy parents. O son of Girisha, considering it well in your mind give up the party of Jambhu's enemy. This Indra himself will sink in deep water, but forsooth before that he will drown you like a heavy boat."

Hearing those words of the Asura Taraka in the battle-field Kartikeya, the son of the three-eyed Siva, with his lips trembling in anger and eyes reddened like a full-blown lotus, cast his looks on his bow and replied :—Yes it becomes you to give vent to such words in pride. I will examine your superior strength of arms; string your bow and take up arrows."

On Kartikeya saying it the Asura, with his lips expanded in anger said :—"If you wish battle being elated with the pride of your strength then bear my arrows bathed in blood." Saying it the king of Asuras immediately stringed his bow, dreadful-looking unto his enemies. Then in anger Kumara set a dreadful looking arrow to his bow resembling a huge serpent. Then stretching his bow to his ears the Daitya-chief discharged arrows. They spread on all sides of his bow. It appeared that the painter of the sky (the sun) was painting arrows on all sides of a mountain with his rays. Covering the celestial army with his shining arrows the Daitya-chief whose shafts strike terror unto heroes was not seen there himself. The various arrows, discharged in battle by the son of Manmatha's enemy drawing his bow to his ear, cut all on a sudden into pieces the shafts of the enemy of gods. Assailing the body of the numerous sky-rangers, and making the day rendered inclement by arrows of the king of Asuras fair he stood there lighting up the world by the irrepressible effulgence of his own person like unto the lord of gods. Then the great Asura-king, Taraka, of fierce energy, in battle more patient, and expert in spreading illusions, began to fight an illusive battle hard to stand. Thereupon when Kumara became victorious in that illusive battle, that highly irrepresible Asura, the flag of victory in the world, seeing his illusion baffled and worked up with anger, laughing hideously put an airy arrow to his bow. As soon as that arrow was shot a terrible wind blew there, causing whirl-winds as at the time of universal dissolution, making a dreadful and hoarse sound raising up dust and covering the middle of the sky and the sun of fierce rays. The wind blew up the umbrellas of the gods white like

Kunda flowers, which flew irregularly in the sky darkened with dust like swans. It also blew up huge flags white like new Mallika flowers at which it appeared that the etherial Ganga was making a thousand of movements. The cars of the celestial host were thrown out of way by that terrible wind. The horses dropped down trembling and the charioteers fled away on all sides in dismay. Trembling, wandering away into wrong tracks and falling down on earth the huge elephants of the army looked like mountains whose wings were cut off by Vasava. When the horses of the celestial host were struck down by that terrible storm, the distressed warriors, throwing off their arms, dropped down on earth as if wounded with weapons. Assailed with that terrific storm the infantry of the gods began to cry distressfully and fearfully. Weapons came out of their hands and fell down on earth at some distance. Thus when the soldiers of the gods were greatly agitated by the king of Daityas with the strokes of his weapons that foremost of gods, Kartikeya, for regaining the prosperity of heaven, began to display a celestial effulgence.

Thereupon united with Kumara and accordingly comforted the soldiers again began to fight. Seeing it the king of Asuras, burning like fire in great anger, discharged a flaming fiery weapon. Thereat obstructing the vision of the gods thick smokes, darkening the ten quarters, black like clouds and shining like lotuses, began to move about in the sky. Seeing the sky covered with darkness setting thick like clouds at the extremities of the quarters as well as with smokes the swans immediately became anxious to go to the lake of Manasa. Then a fire, dreadful like that at the universal dissolution, was ablaze on all sides of the celestial host. Thereat the sky and quarters became red with flames. With continual flames of burning fire and smokes the sky appeared like a row of clouds accompanied with lightnings. Scorched greatly with that unbearable flame moving about in the sky and greatly agitated the celestial host approached the son of Sambhu. Beholding the celestial army thus assailed by fire and overwhelmed Kumara, smiling a little, set an arrow to his bow. Then shaking the mountain summits there arose in sky, muttering terribly, thick clouds dark like darkness, accompanied with the smokes of dissolution. Accompanied with clouds muttering terribly, lightnings, like unto dreadful tongues at the time of universal dissolution, appeared in the sky, lighted up the quarters and ,surprized people. With clouds looking like black throats and like night of dissolution with the rows of teeth, lightnings appeared there as if in terrible rage. Covering the sky and quarters, and assailing the minds with terrible roars clouds began to pour torrents of rain on all sides. When the sky was enshrouded with clouds many rivers of blood flowed in the battle-field, the dead bodies of Asuras striking against their banks. Then the fire spreading to the extremeties of quarters and about to devour the universe was extinguished by rain poured by clouds, covering the sky and destroying many an Asura stricken greatly with the roars of Varuna's weapons.

Thereupon worked up with anger the Asura began to strike Kumara with many razor-shaped arrows discharged from his bow drawn up to ears. The celestials began to fly away on all sides in his fear. Like unto a Yogin destroying worldly objects with infallible rules of self-restraint Kumara, engaged in sport in the battle, cut off into pieces with arrows the bow and shafts of the king of Asuras. Thereupon burning in anger and looking dreadful like a serpent Lord Paramount of the Asuras, Taraka got down from his car, and with leathern fences, and sword in his hands confronted Kumara. Seeing that Asura-chief, having strength of arms invincible unto the soldiers of the gods, approach and looking delightful with a face like unto a lotus the Lord's son, Kartikeya, discharged a huge weapon Sakti capable of consuming everything like the fire of dissolution. Lighting up the sky and the quarters, the great Sakti, accompanied with the tears of grief of the Asuras and tears of joy of the regents of quarters, dropped on the breast of the Asura-chief.

Beholding the Asura Taraka struck down by that Sakti like unto a mountain summit by the wind at the end of a cycle Indra and other gods were filled with delight. Deprived of his life Taraka, the king of the offspring of Danu, fell like a mountain struck by a whirl-wind. With his fangs Ananta, the king of serpents, could with difficulty hold the earth sinking down under the weight of his person. At that time the Kalpa tree, served by black-bees drawn there by perfume, began to shower flowers accompanied with water drops of the celestial river on Shambhu's son Kartikeya the enemy of the Asuras. Thereupon with their faces expanded with joy and bodies filled with delight Indra and other gods, together with the leading celestials, welcomed the strength of Taraka's enemy. Thus when did the son of Smara's enemy, ever victorious in battle, destroyed the king of Danavas, the enemy of the three worlds and like unto a mace, to the abode of death, and when Vala's enemy the king of gods, regained his kingdom in heaven, the celestials bowed unto him touching his foot with their jewelled crests. Released from dangers the gods were crowned with sucess.

---

THE END.